The P9-DCP-528 at

The Food You Want to Eat

100 Smart, Simple Recipes

Ted Allen

with Stephanie Lyness

Photographs by Bill Bettencourt

Clarkson Potter/Publishers
New York

For Barry

Copyright © 2005 by Ted Allen
Photographs copyright © 2005 by Bill Bettencourt

Published in the United States by Clarkson Potter/Publishers,
an imprint of the Crown Publishing Group, a division of
Random House, Inc., New York.
www.clarksonpotter.com

CLARKSON N. POTTER is a trademark and POTTER and colophon are
registered trademarks of Random House, Inc.

Library of Congress Cataloging-in-Publication Data
Allen, Ted.
The food you want to eat: 100 smart, simple recipes / Ted Allen
with Stephanie Lyness.
Includes bibliographical references and index.
1. Cookery.   I. Title.
TX714.A4524   2005
641.5—dc22   2004025653

Printed in China

Design by Helene Silverman

ISBN 1-4000-8090-8

10 9 8 7 6 5 4 3 2 1

First Edition

Contents

Introduction
What you want to eat

With most cookbooks, you could plow through 134 pages of complicated hors d'oeuvres, salads, and the author's endless philosophical musings about food before you get to the stuff you actually want to eat. Not here. I'm going to get to the point right up front. Because my philosophy on these recipes—and the reason for this book—is very simple and very clear: This is smart, cool, easy food, the kind of food that makes people happy. The idea is to inspire people to enjoy cooking and eating as passionately as I do. Whether you're someone who's already adventurous with food, or a regular guy whose primary sustenance is pizza, burgers, and cereal straight out of the box, I have recipes that you'll want to eat. Inspiring and demystifying—that is, simplifying recipes and deflating the pretensiousness of food and wine—have always been my goals on television. That's the plan here, too.

Now, when you're not standing around eating cereal straight out of the box—or even when you are—what is it that you *wish* you were eating? Perfectly grilled steak? Killer mac and cheese? Crispy fried chicken? If it's not one of those comfort-food classics, it's probably something similar. So that's where we begin in this introduction—with the foods I most dearly love to cook and eat, above all others, categories be damned. If you've just recently taken up cooking, maybe something here is where you want to begin. Choose a dish you want to perfect, and go super-easy with the rest of the meal, whether that's just grabbing tossed greens from the grocery-store salad bar, microwaving frozen green beans with cheddar sauce, or baking a potato. If you've got more cooking experience, you could move further into the book—but I'd still encourage you to take a look here. Because throughout, my approach has been to first provide you with a basic recipe—how to pan-fry a steak, say—but then to present several easy variations, ways to elevate the food a little bit, to make it different and more delicious and more interesting. With each successive step-up you take with the dish, whether it's adding a sauce or a Power Butter to that slab of sirloin, or juggling a couple of cool sides from scratch while your date is sipping pinot noir and admiring your artwork, you gain a measure of confidence. And next time, you're turning out food that's better than you ever imagined, without breaking a sweat.

Speaking of sweating: Few things seem to scare your average person more than being called upon to select the "correct" wine, especially if your boss or your date is watching in a restaurant. It doesn't have to be so scary. Matching wines with foods is a somewhat tricky skill to learn, but it's not impossible—it comes through helpful guidance and experience. And I've always appreciated cookbooks that offered wine suggestions. So I've turned to Nancy Maniscalco, owner and missionary of the fantastic wine shop Nancy's Wines for Food on Columbus Avenue in New York City, to provide some pairings for each main dish here. Most dishes offer a couple of wine options, generally one slightly unusual pairing (that, along with affordable wines, is Nancy's stock in trade), and then another that you should be able to locate at any decent wine shop. When in doubt, tell your wine guy what you're cooking, give him a price range, and let him show off his exhaustive knowledge. Later, at your dinner or the next time you're in a restaurant, you can claim to have made the discovery yourself—and you'll be the hero of the table.

Saucepan macaroni and cheese

This stovetop version of mac and cheese is essentially an American *pasta Alfredo*—pasta sauced with a cheesy, creamy sauce, and lots of it—minus the curious orange coloring you get from the notorious blue-boxed version. This is great with Cheddar cheese alone; it's a basic recipe that guarantees you won't alienate any finicky kids or fraternity brothers, should they be on your guest list. But stirring in a couple of tablespoons of Parmigiano-Reggiano cheese—the real stuff, aged and freshly grated, not the kind that comes in a green can—gives this everyman's dish a refinement that will wow gourmet guests, too. A little Colman's hot English mustard, one of my favorites, gives a great little spike of flavor.

SERVES 4 / WINE PAIRING: Light Rosé

Kosher salt for boiling pasta, plus $\frac{1}{2}$ teaspoon for seasoning

1 pound dried macaroni elbows, ziti, or penne

3 tablespoons unsalted butter

3 tablespoons all-purpose flour

3 cups whole milk

$\frac{1}{8}$ teaspoon grated nutmeg

1 bay leaf

2 teaspoons prepared Colman's mustard

8 ounces Cheddar cheese, finely grated

2 tablespoons freshly grated Parmigiano-Reggiano (optional)

$\frac{1}{4}$ teaspoon freshly ground black pepper

> Bring a large, heavy-bottomed pot of salted water (1 teaspoon of salt per quart) to a boil. Add the pasta and cook until it's al dente, more than likely about 8 minutes. Drain it in a colander.

> Return the pot to low heat and melt the butter in it. Add the flour and whisk for 1 minute, until the mixture bubbles. Raise the heat to medium. Gradually add the milk, whisking all the time to blend. Then add the nutmeg and bay leaf and bring to a simmer, whisking constantly, particularly at the edges of the pot. When the sauce simmers it will thicken. Turn the heat down to low and cook at a bare simmer for 10 minutes; this cooks away the floury taste.

> Remove the pan from the heat. Discard the bay leaf. Stir in the mustard. Now add the drained pasta and the grated cheeses. Put the pan over very low heat and stir to melt the cheese. Season with $\frac{1}{4}$ teaspoon salt and $\frac{1}{4}$ teaspoon pepper. Spoon out into a serving bowl, or onto serving plates, and serve immediately.

Simplest roast chicken with lemon and herbs

After much experimentation, I've come up with this recipe as the simplest, most effective way to make a great-tasting bird with crisp skin and a minimum of hassle. That said, I want to encourage you *not* to follow my recipe. Okay; follow the actual roasting technique. But beyond that, use what you have got in your refrigerator.

For example: I wrote this recipe with tarragon because I love that herb, and because I've been overdosing on rosemary lately. But if you made White Bean Purée (page 32) a couple of days ago, chances are you have got leftover sage in your refrigerator. Under no circumstances should you rush out to your supermarket to buy tarragon when you already have sage. Got an onion but no garlic . . . ? Get the picture? Remember, this is a roast chicken, not brain surgery.

SERVES 4 / WINE PAIRING: Crisp unoaked Chardonnay, Chablis, or Cabarnet Franc

$3/4$ teaspoon plus 1 pinch kosher or sea salt

$1/4$ teaspoon plus 1 pinch freshly ground black pepper

1 4-pound chicken, rinsed inside and out and patted dry with paper towels

$1/2$ lemon

$1/2$ head of garlic

1 bay leaf

1 bunch of fresh tarragon

4 tablespoons ($1/2$ stick) unsalted butter

$1/2$ cup white wine or water, if needed

1 medium shallot, chopped or sliced—whatever's easiest

1 cup canned low-sodium chicken stock

> Preheat the oven to 400°F. Put a roasting pan with a rack (preferably a V-shaped rack—see Note) in there to heat up.

> In a small bowl, stir together the salt and pepper. Cut off any lumps of fat you see around the neck of the chicken. Then balance the bird on the neck end and sprinkle the inside of the cavity with about half of the salt and pepper mixture. Put the lemon half into the cavity, along with the garlic, bay leaf, and about three quarters of the tarragon. Sprinkle the outside of the chicken with the remaining salt and pepper.

> Melt 2 tablespoons of the butter. (Just stick it in a microwaveable container and microwave for about 30 seconds—but pull it out the second it looks melted, so it doesn't pop and make a mess.) From the remaining tarragon sprigs, chop 1 table-spoon of leaves and set aside. Reserve a few sprigs for garnishing, if you like.

> When you're ready with the chicken, open the oven and pull out the oven rack supporting the roasting pan. Put the chicken, breast side down, on the V-rack and pour over about half of the melted butter. Now close the oven door and roast for 40 minutes. Using tongs (hook them into the cavity), turn the bird, breast side up, and pour the remaining butter over the breast. Continue roasting until an instant-

read thermometer inserted into the thickest part of the thigh reads 165° to 170°F., 35 to 40 minutes longer, or about 1 hour and 15 to 1 hour and 20 minutes total cooking time. Check after about 50 minutes to 1 hour, to see if the stuff at the bottom of the pan is beginning to burn. If so, add about 1/2 cup white wine or water. When the chicken is cooked, put it on a plate and let it rest while you make the sauce.

> Remove the V-rack from the pan and put the pan over medium heat. Cook for a couple of minutes until the juices reduce and caramelize on the bottom and you're left with a little fat. You want about 2 tablespoons of fat. Get rid of the rest with a spoon, or just pour it out. Add the shallot and cook, stirring, until translucent, about 1 minute. Add the chicken stock and reduce by about half, 4 to 5 minutes. Pour any juices that have accumulated on the plate with the chicken into the pan, too. Add the reserved chopped tarragon and the remaining 2 tablespoons of butter and stir that in until the butter melts and the sauce thickens. Add a pinch of salt and pepper.

> To portion the bird, cut it into quarters: Cut between the leg and breast on each side, then down through the hip joints to cut off the legs. Cut along each side of the breastbone, then push the breast halves off the carcass. Spoon the sauce over the meat and decorate the plates with the tarragon sprigs, if using.

NOTE: Bottom line: If you want crisp skin, you need a V-rack. This is a relatively inexpensive piece of equipment, shaped like a V, that keeps the bird off the bottom of the pan and so lets the heat really get in there to crisp the skin. Oil the rack so that the skin doesn't stick.

+ *VARIATION:* **White Wine Sauce**
Before you add the chicken stock to make the sauce, pour in about 1/2 cup whatever white wine you're drinking that night and cook it down by about half, about 3 minutes. Then continue with the recipe.

+ *VARIATION:* **Red Wine Sauce**
For Francophiles. Sauté the shallot as in the recipe. Now add 1/2 cup red wine (a Côtes du Rhône or Pinot Noir works very well) and cook it down by half, about 1 minute. Stir in 1/2 cup stock, preferably the thicker, darker *glace de viande* (sold by D'Artagnan and distributed nationally) that you've purchased frozen at a gourmet grocer or butcher. Pour in any juices that have accumulated on the plate with the chicken. Simmer that all together for a couple of minutes and finish with the butter and tarragon.

+ *VARIATION:* **No Sauce at All**
Serve with lemon or lime wedges, drizzle with olive oil, and extol the virtues of simplicity to your dinner guests.

the essentials of steak
Given the choice, I like my steaks grilled. And grilled over charcoal, in the backyard, while I'm enjoying a cold Sierra Nevada Pale Ale. There's just no substitute for that charred, smoky flavor, or for the crispy crust you can achieve on the truly hot barbecue. But you might be surprised to learn that a good piece of steak is going to taste great cooked on your stovetop, too.

Perhaps the most important element of a great steak, aside from the quality of the meat (read about that below), is the crust. If you don't get a well-browned exterior, you lose texture and caramelized flavor. You end up with a piece of meat that tastes more boiled or stewed than grilled or sautéed. We call this technique of browning the outside of the meat "searing." A lot of people believe that searing meat seals in the juices; personally, I don't think it makes much difference on that score. But there's no question that searing is crucial

Another crucial element is knowing when the thing is done. This is largely a question of experience. I do suggest cooking times for steaks in these recipes, but there are so many variables: the heat of your burner or fire; the thickness of the steak; the temperature of the steak when you start cooking it; the weather, if you're outside. Your best bet is to check on your food as you go. Eventually, you may learn to judge the doneness of steak just by feel; a rare steak is soft and jiggly, while an overcooked steak is much firmer. In your beginnings as a Lord of the Grill, though, you'll probably need to make little cuts into your steak to check on what's happening inside. Don't worry about it; one little peek inside is not going to drain your dinner of all its juiciness. (Here's a hint: Buy steaks that are all the same thickness, so you only need to cut one of them. This should be the one you eat yourself, so your guests won't feel that their meat has been violated.)

Then, remember to take the steak off when it still looks a little less cooked than you want. Steaks, chops, and roasts need to "rest" after cooking—that means letting them sit for a few minutes (in a warmish place, maybe under some foil) to allow the juices to redistribute throughout the meat. During this time, the steak will also become a little more done; if you take a steak off the grill at a perfect medium, it may be medium well by the time it has rested.

CHOICE CUTS

My favorite steak is the bone-in rib eye they serve at Gibson's Steakhouse in Chicago. I once wrote in "Chicago" magazine that the prodigious piece of beef looks more like a weapon than an entrée, because the rib bone could be a handle, and the meaty part is shaped like an ax blade. But then, there's the magnificent porterhouse—the best of both worlds, with the T-shaped bone separating the filet from the strip steak. And on the humbler end of the Angus, there's the brisket—you haven't lived until you've tasted Ray Green's brisket down at North Main BBQ in Dallas. Come to think of it, I love virtually every kind of beef, and each has its merits. They may have different names depending on what part of the country you're from and how your butcher likes to carve and name them, but here are the beefy basics:

PRIME RIB: A boneless steak; may be called Delmonico. A particularly rich cut with lots of visible pieces of fat; very tender, almost silky texture; good flavor. You can buy it on or off the bone.

STRIP STEAK: Also called New York strip, shell, or top loin. Lovely, meaty texture; medium rich, great flavor. Available on or off the bone.

PORTERHOUSE: For people who want it all, this cut includes both a piece of strip steak and, on the other side of the bone, a good-size round of tenderloin.

T-BONE: Like a porterhouse, but with a smaller piece of tenderloin. The strip is said to be more tender than on a porterhouse because it is close to the ribs, but I can't tell the difference.

TENDERLOIN: Often served as an entire filet or as filet mignon (beef medallions). A very tender, lean piece of meat, with very mild flavor. Really benefits from a creamy sauce.

HANGER STEAK: A great steak that your butcher has but that you probably don't know about. This is a long, slender piece of meat, usually about 1 inch thick, that looks a lot like a pork tenderloin, only redder. Lean, with a rich, beefy taste. Some people find it a little touchy to cook, but I don't find it any trickier than a tenderloin. Grill it for 6 to 7 minutes total, just to medium rare; any rarer than that and it's tough. Overcook it and it's dry.

QUALITY

You're going to hear different things about quality of meat these days. It used to be that "quality" meant the meat that had the most marbling—fat that runs through the muscle and melts into it as it cooks, keeping the meat tender and succulent. This meat was graded "prime"; meat with less marbling was "choice"; and anything lesser was destined for stew.

The other marker of the best steak was that it be dry-aged: aged in a refrigerated environment for a number of weeks (three to four weeks, or even up to six) so that the meat loses some of its moisture and the fat and flavor become concentrated, resulting in a very tender, rich-tasting steak. Meat is now often wet-aged (aged for several weeks in plastic).

These days, of course, fat is not necessarily desirable. So a lot of butchers are selling "choice" as the preferable grade, and organic and free-range meats are often bred to choice standards. If you have a butcher who's selling dry-aged prime steak, taste it against the wet-aged choice. The dry-aged will cost you an arm and a leg: you'll probably spend sixteen to eighteen dollars on one steak alone. But you'll taste the difference.

Grilled steak

Fire it up, folks! Grilled steak is one of my favorites. It's also one of the easiest things to cook, which is probably why it's the one thing everybody's father is willing to cook. If you want porterhouse, buy two thick steaks for four people, and carve them at the table. (They are such large beasts that they must be cut very thin to serve only one person—and that sort of takes the fun out of things.) Of course, serve this meat with potatoes, like the potato gratin on page 164.

A note on stocking steaks for dinner: These days, many people (especially small women and the nutrition police) are satisfied with a 6- to 10-ounce serving of beef, with side dishes, of course. But hearty eaters will demand more. It's always better to have some leftovers than to leave people hungry.

$3/4$ teaspoon kosher salt

$3/4$ teaspoon freshly ground black pepper

4 excellent steaks (rib-eye, T-bone, or strip), with or without bone
   ($1^{1}/_{4}$ to $1^{1}/_{2}$ inches thick), or 2 porterhouse steaks ($1^{1}/_{2}$ inches thick)

> The first thing you need to do is to build your fire. Dump a bunch of briquettes on one side *only* of your grill, so that you have a pile that reaches a couple of inches below the grilling grate. Light the briquettes and let them burn until completely covered with gray ash. This will take from 20 to 30 minutes, depending on whether you're using charcoal briquettes (30 minutes) or hardwood charcoal (only about 20 minutes).

> Use a piece of metal fireplace equipment, such as tongs or a shovel, to scrape some of the coals off the pile onto the empty side of the grill so that you have one side that's very hot, and another side that's not so hot. Use the hand test to judge when your coals are hot enough: When you can hold your hand 5 inches above the grill for only 5 to 6 seconds before it starts to hurt, that's low heat; 3 to 4 seconds, that's medium; 2 seconds, that's *hot*. (Um, as soon as it starts to hurt, pull back your paw, please.)

> In a small bowl, combine the salt and pepper. Lay your steaks on a cutting board and sprinkle both sides with the seasoning. Put the steaks on the hotter part of the grill until they develop a really good crust (if you're cooking on a gas grill you may have to content yourself with grill marks in lieu of a real crust); this should only take 2 to 3 minutes. No need to be concerned about a little bit of flare-up; this helps form the crust. (If it gets out of control, though, you can calm the fire down by closing the lid or spraying the coals with a squirt gun.) Turn the steaks with tongs, and brown the other side, another 2 to 3 minutes. Now pull the steaks over to the cooler side of the grill and continue cooking until they're done to your liking: For $1^{1}/_{2}$-inch cuts, 7 to 8 minutes total gives you medium rare. (Grill a little less for rare, a little more for medium.)

> Let the steaks rest for about 5 minutes before you cut into them—this is essential!— to give the juices a chance to redistribute through the meat. Serve with one of the Power Butters on page 136, crumbled Maytag Blue Cheese with Parsley and Peppercorns (page 137), or just a drizzle of excellent extra-virgin olive oil.

Red-wine braised short ribs

Beef short ribs make a fantastic stew because they've got so much taste and cook into an ultra-tender, velvety texture. Short ribs are just the top 4 to 5 inches of the prime rib bones. The vegetables can all be chopped in a food processor, making the preparation quick and easy. And then the braising itself—letting the meat slowly bubble away in liquid for hours—may be the easiest possible cooking method when you've got guests coming: for one, it requires practically no attention while it's on the stove; the cooking time is totally flexible, so there's no need to set a timer or worry about doing anything at precisely 6:27; braising fills your home with utterly irresistible aromas; and nearly all braised dishes, including this one, are actually *better* the second day, so you can make this entire dish in advance, refrigerate, and just reheat before serving. Paired up with some egg noodles tossed in a little butter, dinner couldn't be easier. Or tastier.

SERVES 4 / WINE PAIRING: Côtes du Rhône or Cabernet Sauvignon

1 large onion, quartered

4 medium carrots, cut into 2-inch lengths

1 celery stalk, cut into 2-inch lengths

10 fresh parsley sprigs

$3^1/2$ pounds beef short ribs

$1^1/2$ teaspoons salt, plus more to taste

$1/2$ teaspoon freshly ground black pepper, plus more to taste

1 tablespoon extra-virgin olive oil

4 garlic cloves, smashed

1 bottle (750 ml) full-bodied but not terribly expensive red wine such as
    cabernet sauvignon, merlot, or Côtes du Rhône

1 sprig fresh oregano

2 bay leaves

> Put the onion, carrots, and celery in a food processor and pulse to coarsely chop. Don't worry if you're left with one or two large pieces of carrot—the stew will cook long enough to cook everything. Pull the leaves off the parsley sprigs. Chop the leaves and set them aside; rinse the stems and set them aside too.

> Put the ribs on a large plate and sprinkle with $1^1/2$ teaspoons salt and $1/2$ teaspoon pepper. Heat the oil in a Dutch oven or large pot over a medium-high flame. Add the seasoned short ribs and brown on all sides, 12 to 15 minutes. Don't let the bottom of the pot burn; if it begins to burn, turn down the heat. Remove the meat back to the plate with tongs or a slotted spoon. You should have 1 to 2 tablespoons fat left in the pot; that's perfect. If you have more, throw off the excess to leave a generous tablespoon.

> Turn the heat down to medium. Add the chopped vegetables and the garlic and cook, stirring, 8 to 10 minutes, until the onions are translucent and may be beginning to brown. (It's nice if they brown, but not important.)

> Add the wine and bring to a simmer, scraping the bottom of the pot with a wooden spoon to pull up any browned bits that are still stuck there. Return the ribs to the pan along with any juices that have collected on the plate while they sat there. Add the parsley stems, the oregano, and bay leaves. Add enough water to barely cover the meat (another 2 to 3 cups should do it). Turn the heat down to low, partially cover, and cook until the meat is very soft and falling off the bone, about $2\frac{1}{2}$ hours. Turn the ribs a few times while they cook (if you remember). And check during the last hour of cooking to see how the sauce is doing. You want it to reduce and thicken enough to make a very thin gravy. (Figure that it will reduce by about half, so that if you stick a spoon into the sauce, the liquid will very thinly coat the back of the spoon.) If it's reducing very slowly, take off the lid and let the stew cook uncovered for a while.

> When the stew is done and you like the look of the sauce, stir in the chopped parsley and taste for salt and pepper. Serve in deep plates over a bed of buttered egg noodles.

Fried chicken

Here's the trick: Soak your chicken. In buttermilk. Maybe it tenderizes the meat, maybe it doesn't, but one thing's for certain: the sugar in the buttermilk is great for flavor and browning. And its thick, gluey consistency assures that when you roll the chicken pieces in flour, lots of the flour will stick; that batter is what gets you a great crust. I don't find it necessary to completely submerge the chicken in hot oil—a messy proposition, that deep-frying approach. Really, ½ inch in your frying pan is quite enough for digit-lickin' results.

This recipe is immeasurably better if you can let the chicken marinate overnight; the garlic and thyme infuse the bird with flavor, and the salty marinade also assures moist meat. The dish will still work if you don't have that marinating time, but if you can plan ahead enough, and take 15 minutes to prep the day before, you'll be really happy about it when you're chomping on that drumstick.

1½ cups buttermilk

1 tablespoon plus 1½ teaspoons kosher salt

1½ teaspoons freshly ground black pepper

6 medium garlic cloves, smashed

1 tablespoon roughly chopped fresh thyme leaves (just give them a whack or
    two to bruise them and release the flavor)

1 3½- to 4-pound chicken, cut into 8 pieces, rinsed and patted dry

1 quart canola oil

2 cups all-purpose flour

> In a large bowl, combine the buttermilk with 1 tablespoon of the salt, 1 teaspoon of the pepper, the garlic, and thyme. Add the chicken, cover, and refrigerate for at least a couple of hours, or preferably overnight.

> In a large frying pan or Dutch oven—something that can be covered—heat about ½ inch oil over a medium-high flame to 350° to 375°F. on a deep-fry thermometer. (A 13-inch straight-sided frying pan is perfect.)

> Meanwhile, combine the flour with the remaining 1½ teaspoons salt and ½ teaspoon pepper in a heavy resealable plastic bag. Working with 2 or 3 pieces at a time, take the chicken out of the buttermilk, put it in the bag, close the bag, and shake well to coat the chicken with the flour. Put the chicken on a baking sheet.

> When the oil is hot, carefully place the chicken into the pan with tongs, skin side down. If using a 13-inch pan, just cram the pieces in—don't worry about it, you can rearrange later. The important thing is to get them in before hot oil splatters all over you. If using a smaller pot or a Dutch oven, cook the chicken in 2 batches. Cover, and cook 5 minutes. Then uncover the pan and cook until the skin is nicely browned, 5 more minutes. Turn the chicken and continue to cook until well browned and cooked through, 6 to 8 more minutes for the breast meat, 8 to 10 more minutes for the dark meat. If the chicken starts to brown too quickly, turn the heat down a little.

> Line the baking sheet with a double layer of paper towels and drain the chicken on the towels. Serve immediately, at room temperature, or cold.

+ *VARIATION:* Spicy Fried Chicken
Season the flour with 2 teaspoons chili powder, 2 teaspoons ground cumin, and ¼ teaspoon cayenne (omit the cayenne if you want spice flavor but not heat).

Warm caramel brownie sundaes

Hot homemade brownies with a great gooey caramel sauce and a scoop of vanilla ice cream—it doesn't get more irresistible. The brownies are buttery, chocolaty, and just sweet enough. The whole thing can be made ahead, and the brownies can be re-heated for 30 to 60 seconds in your microwave; the sauce reheats easily over low heat.

SERVES 4

for the brownies

4 ounces (1 stick) unsalted butter, at room temperature, plus more for greasing the pan

3 ounces bittersweet chocolate, coarsely chopped

$3/4$ cup sugar

1 teaspoon pure vanilla extract

3 large eggs

$1/2$ cup all-purpose flour

for the caramel sauce

1 cup sugar

$1/2$ cup heavy cream

1 teaspoon pure vanilla extract

for serving

$1/2$ cup pecan pieces

1 pint good-quality vanilla ice cream (I'm partial to Häagen-Dazs)

> To make the brownies, preheat the oven to 350°F. Butter an 8 × 8-inch baking dish.

> Put the chocolate in a heat-proof glass bowl, cover with plastic wrap or a paper towel, and microwave at 30-second intervals until just melted, 1 to 3 minutes depending on your microwave. Or, if you don't have a microwave, bring about 1 inch water to a simmer in the bottom of a double boiler or in a saucepan into which another pan will fit without touching the water. Put the chocolate in the top of the double boiler or in the top pan, and let the water simmer until the chocolate melts, 2 to 3 minutes; remove from the heat and set aside.

> In a mixing bowl, beat the butter with the sugar until creamy and light colored. Add the melted chocolate and the vanilla extract and stir until smooth. In a small bowl, beat the eggs with a fork. Pour the eggs into the chocolate mixture and blend well. Stir in the flour. Pour the batter into the prepared baking dish and bake on the middle rack until a knife inserted into the center of the brownies comes out not quite clean, about 25 minutes. Let cool for about 10 minutes.

> While the brownies bake, make the caramel sauce. Put the sugar and $\frac{1}{2}$ cup water in a nonaluminum saucepan over low heat. Cook, stirring, until the sugar is dissolved (the liquid will look clear), 1 to 2 minutes. Turn the heat up to medium and cook without stirring until the liquid—called a sugar syrup—turns a caramel color, about 20 minutes. (You'll see the syrup develop big, slow-breaking bubbles as the water boils away, and then it will begin to darken around the edges of the pan. Swirl the pan a little for even cooking.)

> When the syrup has turned a dark amber color, remove the pan from the heat and immediately pour in the cream. Stand back; the caramel will sputter. Stir to combine. (The sauce will be lumpy—that's normal. The caramel hardens on contact with the cream.) Return to low heat to melt the caramel and cook until smooth. Remove from the heat and stir in the vanilla.

> While the oven is still hot, spread the pecans out on a baking sheet and toast until fragrant, about 10 minutes.

> To serve, cut four 4-inch brownies and place each in a shallow bowl or deep plate. Add a couple of scoops of ice cream. Pour some of the sauce over and sprinkle with the nuts.

1 / **Happy hour**

This book is not about throwing ultra-formal dinners, so we're not getting into a bunch of recipes for fancy canapés, followed by appetizers, followed by soup, etc., etc. That said, you do have to give people something when they walk in the door; it takes the edge off their appetite and makes them feel at home. And when you're older than twenty-one and are offering adult beverages, it's nice to accompany those drinks with something besides Doritos. Food, particularly rich food, keeps the body from metabolizing alcohol instantaneously, and thus helps your guests remain upright through cocktail hour. It's also just not civilized to serve drinks without nibblies.

There's more to appreciate about cocktail hour than the bare essentials of liquids and solids. Some people I know have elevated the ritual to an art form, with groovy glassware, linens, and accessories. As a guest at a couple's house in Mobile, Alabama, for cocktails several years ago, I developed an appreciation for drinking out of cut crystal rocks glasses. They feel solid, hefty, and luxurious; they positively glitter with elegance. My hosts were seasoned pros at entertaining, and, in addition to the great glassware, they also sported some serious silver and a great recipe for pickled crabmeat. The fine details really enhance the experience.

We don't need to get into a major treatise on entertaining, but you do want some tricks up your sleeve if you're going to have people over *and* enjoy yourself. So this chapter offers recipes for ten cocktails that you absolutely must know how to make—five classics, five originals—along with some great snacks to accompany them. All of the food can be made ahead (to some extent, at least, even if it must be assembled at the last minute) and served cold or popped in the oven when people arrive. Cheers!

Herbed parmesan crisps

This is the easiest homemade cocktail snack you could ever imagine. Even better, it's probably the most delicious one in existence—salty, cheesy, and irresistible. It's basically a *very* cheesy cheese cracker; just a bit of shredded cheese baked with a tiny bit of flour and some herbs until it's good and crispy. (It has the added advantage of making your house smell fantastic.) It's also a great-tasting and beautiful addition to a salad.

MAKES 12 CRISPS

1 cup finely shredded Parmesan cheese, preferably Parmigiano-Reggiano

2 teaspoons all-purpose flour

1 teaspoon finely chopped fresh rosemary or thyme

$1/4$ teaspoon freshly ground black pepper

> Preheat the oven to 350°F.

> In a small bowl, mix all the ingredients together. On a baking sheet coated lightly with cooking spray or lined with parchment paper, place tablespoonfuls of the mixture with a couple inches between each, and spread them out into ovals about 4 inches long and 2 wide. (You should have about 12 crisps.) Bake in the oven until they turn golden brown, 6 to 8 minutes. Cool the crisps flat on a metal rack.

Cucumber yogurt dip

A refreshing, cool counterpoint to your salty crispy cocktail snacks. Serve with pita bread, pita chips, or veggies.

MAKES ABOUT 2 CUPS

1 English cucumber (the long skinny type, usually wrapped in plastic)

$1/2$ teaspoon kosher salt

2 cups yogurt, preferably thick Greek yogurt (see Note)

2 sprigs of fresh dill, chopped

$1^{1/2}$ tablespoons chopped fresh mint leaves

$1/2$ teaspoon ground cumin (optional)

$1/8$ teaspoon freshly ground black pepper

Extra-virgin olive oil, for drizzling

> Peel the cucumber and cut it in half lengthwise. Then use a spoon to scoop out and discard the seeds from both halves. Grate the cucumber on the wide holes of a grater, put it in a colander in the sink, and sprinkle with the salt. Let drain for about 20 minutes, then press with your hands to get rid of more of the moisture.

> In a medium bowl, stir the grated cucumber into the yogurt along with the dill, mint, cumin (if using), and pepper. Chill. Drizzle with about 1 teaspoon oil before serving.

NOTE: Greek cow's-milk or sheep's-milk yogurt, sold at many gourmet shops, is a completely different yogurt than the stuff you're probably used to. It's very thick, very creamy (even the low-fat varieties), and very good. It's worth the hunt.

✳ How to put together a cocktail party

There are no hard and fast rules, except maybe this one: Get a drink into your guests' hands within five minutes of their arrival. And this one: Put the food at one end of the room, and the drinks at the other. This promotes traffic flow and reduces clumping and lines. And definitely this one: Never, ever allow the music to stop.

I guess there are a few hard and fast rules.

A smart way for the novice entertainer to give a cocktail party and keep his workload and expenses down is to declare a theme: a margarita party, for instance. That way you know what you're serving, you buy *only* that, and you don't open a whole bunch of bottles for one drink apiece. And in my experience, people really like a theme.

If you don't want to go that route, settle on a small selection of drinks. Plan on two to three drinks per person and at least three quarters of a pound of ice per person. Choose three to four liquors, such as vodka, gin, and bourbon, and three mixers: cranberry, orange, and tonic, as well as a couple kinds of soft drinks. Buy mixers such as tonic and soda in small bottles—less waste, more fizz. One medium-priced red and one medium-priced white wine are useful, too. Lemons and limes and good quality green olives round out your basic garnishing needs, although having mint and rosemary handy would give you some more stylish and interesting options.

And then there's ambiance: Dim the lights a little, light a few candles, fill a vase with a few fresh flowers—done.

the antipasto platter

In Italy, antipasto simply means "before the meal" and can consist of any number of appetizers. An antipasto platter—typically a collection of cured meats, cheeses, and olives for starters, and perhaps some pickled vegetables such as peppers, mushrooms, or eggplant—is probably the coolest, simplest, and most elegant finger food you can serve.

One of the advantages of the antipasto platter is that you needn't actually *cook* anything. Find a decent Italian deli or a gourmet store that sells imported French or Greek or Middle Eastern foods and you'll be all set. (Another advantage is that you are obliged to taste a lot of different meats and cheeses to determine what you want to serve; many stores will give you tastes.) Some supermarkets have a pretty decent "gourmet" department for this sort of thing as well.

For four people, plan to serve three to four different cheeses, three to four different meats (four ounces total protein per person), a selection of olives, and a good-quality dense bread—sliced —with olive oil or butter. Beyond that you can add anything else you like: roasted peppers; those leftover roasted root vegetables in the refrigerator; thin slices of ripe melon and/or whole, ripe figs; raw vegetables; or some good-quality pickled or marinated vegetables. Even a mound of yesterday's egg salad.

When you choose your cheese, try to offer a variety of taste and texture. Think about combining cow's, sheep's, and goat's milk cheeses, each of which has a unique taste. You might serve one hard, sharp cheese such as Provolone, or Pecorino (sheep's milk), or a fresh Parmigiano. Then, a softer, more delicate cheese such as a Fontina, or a ripe, soft French cheese. (Camembert and Brie are, of course, the best known of this type but there are many more, such as the delectable Epoisses.) Add a fresh or dry French goat cheese, an Italian (Gorgonzola) or French (Bleu d'Auvergne) blue cheese, or a Greek or French feta. You can probably find little balls of mozzarella (bocconcini) marinated in olive oil, balsamic vinegar, and red pepper flakes, even at your supermarket.

A tremendous variety of French- and Italian-style cured meats and sausages are available. Even at the supermarket you can find dried cured salami such as Genoa salami and pepperoni, among others. It's also possible these days to buy very good imported cured ham from Italy (prosciutto) and Spain (jamón de Serrano), as well as air-dried beef (bresaola). Domestic Smithfield ham has a different taste entirely. Grab a few of your old faves, but also try new things while you're putting the platter together.

And finally, think about having a variety of color and texture as you pick things to go on the plate. Food should be as beautiful as it is delicious.

Rosemary marinated olives

I can't have cocktail hour without great, fresh olives — and I don't mean the rubbery, tasteless black ones from a can. I mean the real deal: kalamatas, niçoises, gaetas, picholines — the more variety, the better. Most good supermarkets these days feature an olive bar — that is, a variety of loose olives available in bulk. Some of these places include among the selection a batch of olives that have been seasoned with herbs and other flavors, too. But it's more fun to do it yourself: You can buy different kinds of olives (be sure to get different sizes and colors, which looks great in the bowl), select the flavors you like the best — say, thyme, cayenne, garlic, grapefruit zest, whatever — and you can control the spiciness. You'll have a great collection of olives for your next impromptu get-together, or an excellent addition to an antipasto platter (see opposite). And they're almost no work at all to make.

When you serve, remember to put out a small dish so guests have someplace to put the pits.

MAKES 1 POUND

1 pound mixed olives
2 strips of lemon zest
1 tablespoon fresh rosemary needles
A couple sprigs of fresh thyme
1 medium garlic clove
$\frac{1}{2}$ cup extra-virgin olive oil

> Combine the olives, lemon zest, rosemary, and thyme in an attractive jar that has a cover. Bury the garlic clove in the center, add the oil, stir, cover, and refrigerate until you need it, up to several weeks. Give the mixture another stir now and then to blend. And try other flavors: herbs such as tarragon, other citrus peels, chilies, seasoned oils — whatever you like.

Spicy cajun "pigs" in puff pastry

This is a great example of a way to take a comfort-food classic (in this case, the "pigs-in-a-blanket" traditionally made with hot dogs and crescent-roll dough) and reinterpret it in a new, more interesting way. They're perfect for game day or parties, they're excellent warm or cold, and they smell as great as they look. I first served these to the brothers of Sigma Chi at the University of North Texas outside Dallas during a particularly adventuresome episode of *Queer Eye,* and they earned a unanimous review of "Bad-ass!" Then, the brothers figured out the recipe, made an assembly line, and whipped up enough of these things to serve sixty people.

Serve with plain mustard or with the chutney mustard below.

MAKES ABOUT 42 PIECES; SERVES ABOUT 10 PARTYGOERS

1 package (1.1 pounds) frozen puff pastry
All-purpose flour, for rolling
2 large eggs, whisked with a fork, for glazing
1 pound andouille or other spicy cooked sausage, sliced crosswise
about $1/3$ inch thick

chutney mustard

$1/2$ cup Dijon mustard
$1/2$ cup Major Grey's chutney (sold in the condiments aisle)

> Thaw the pastry overnight in the refrigerator if you remember, or at least 1 hour at room temperature before you plan to use it.

> Preheat the oven to 425°F.

> Flour a work surface. Place one sheet of dough on the work surface and roll it out to a rectangle that measures $14^1/2$ inches wide on the top and bottom edges by $13^1/2$ inches on the sides. Cut the rectangle crosswise into 3 strips, $14^1/2$ inches long by $4^1/2$ inches wide. Set two of the strips aside.

> Cut the pastry strip you're working with into triangles: see the diagram.

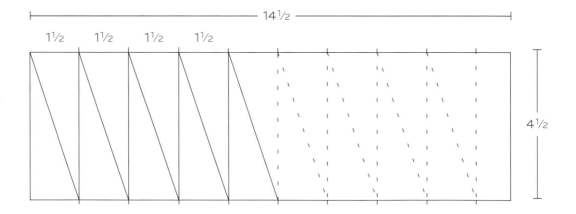

> Cut a sheet of parchment paper (see Note) about the size of a baking sheet. Put all of the dough triangles on the parchment-lined pan. Brush the dough triangles with the egg glaze. Now put one of the andouille slices at the wide end of one of the triangles, about 1/3 inch down from the top. Fold the top of the dough up to cover the side of the sausage slice, then roll the slice over, with the dough, and then over again, so that you've now wrapped the sausage slice in the dough and the pointy end is on top. Continue in the same way to use all of the dough triangles. Brush the rolled pastry with egg glaze.

> Continue in the same way, cutting the remaining strips of dough into triangles and wrapping the sausage slices. Use more parchment-lined pans as you need to. Then bake the triangles until the pastry is golden brown, about 15 minutes.

> Meanwhile, stir together the mustard and chutney.

> When the pastries are cooked, remove them to a paper towel to drain (the andouille is rich). Then arrange them on a platter and serve with the chutney mustard.

NOTE: Why you need parchment paper: because it means virtually zero cleanup. Lining a baking sheet with parchment prevents cookies, pigs-in-a-blanket, breads, etc., from sticking to the sheet. You can find it next to the foil in the grocery store.

✷ Cheesy pastry snacks

Don't even think about throwing away that extra puff pastry.

When you make the spicy Cajun pigs, above, you'll notice that each package of puff pastry contains 2 sheets of pastry; you'll get about 42 triangles from each sheet. One pound of sausage will yield about 48 slices. So unless you're doubling the recipe to feed half the French Quarter, you'll have a sheet of puff pastry left over. Here is a spectacularly delicious and easy use for that sheet:

Glaze the rest of the dough with the remaining egg glaze and sprinkle with 1/2 cup finely grated Gruyère cheese and 1/2 cup grated Parmigiano-Reggiano cheese. Cut the dough into 2-inch squares, or, if you like, into long, 1-inch strips that you can then twist into "straws." Bake at 425°F. on a parchment-lined baking sheet until browned and puffed, 12 to 15 minutes; serve them directly from the oven. These make fabulous cocktail-hour hors d'oeuvres.

Crostini

Crostini are the essence of rustic Italian snacking; nothing could be easier or more crowd-pleasing. Make a few of the different varieties, and you'll also notice how beautiful crostini look on big platters—that is, for the brief interval before they're all eaten.

MAKES 30 TO 35 PIECES

1 good-quality baguette
Extra-virgin olive oil

> Preheat the oven to 400°F.

> Cut the baguette into thin slices on an angle, lay them on baking sheets, and drizzle with olive oil. Bake until the crostini are beginning to brown and crisp, 10 to 12 minutes. Serve with some or all of the following dips and spreads.

oven-dried tomatoes

You have to try this; tomatoes that have been dried in the oven take on a very different, more intense flavor than raw tomatoes. Roasting them slowly dehydrates the flesh, concentrating the flavors and making them sweeter. These are much fresher and softer than prepackaged sun-dried tomatoes, which tend to be too chewy for some uses.

MAKES ABOUT 2 CUPS

2 pounds Roma or plum tomatoes
1 teaspoon kosher salt
2 tablespoons chopped fresh thyme, marjoram, or oregano
1$\frac{1}{2}$ tablespoons extra-virgin olive oil

> Preheat the oven to 250°F.

> Cut the tomatoes in half lengthwise, then squeeze them, cut sides down, over a sink to get rid of the seeds. Place them cut sides up on a baking sheet. Sprinkle with the salt and herbs and drizzle with the olive oil. Put the tomatoes in the oven and let them dry out very slowly until the flavor has concentrated and they're wrinkly but still plump, 3$\frac{1}{2}$ to 4 hours. Let them cool, then use immediately, or pack them in a jar with olive oil to cover; they will keep for up to 2 weeks.

white bean purée

It's a Tuscan thing. And if you haven't been to Tuscany—a beautiful, rolling province of Italy a few clicks north of Rome—you should put it on your list. Great food, great people—and, it must be noted, great shopping. (See my website, www.tedallen.net, for directions to the outlet stores for Prada *and* Gucci. Seriously.)

MAKES ABOUT 2 CUPS

1 can (19 ounces) white cannellini beans, drained and rinsed (about 1½ cups)
5 tablespoons extra-virgin olive oil, plus more for drizzling
1 medium garlic clove
1 tablespoon fresh lemon juice (from about ½ lemon)
1 teaspoon chopped fresh sage
Dash of hot sauce
⅛ teaspoon kosher salt, plus more to taste
¼ teaspoon freshly ground black pepper

optional garnishes

1 tablespoon chopped flat-leaf parsley
Leaves from 1 sprig of basil, chopped
¼ teaspoon ground cumin or paprika
¼ cup chopped or sliced very sweet cherry or grape tomatoes

> Combine the beans, 5 tablespoons oil, garlic, lemon juice, sage, hot sauce, ⅛ teaspoon salt, and ¼ teaspoon pepper in a food processor and purée. Scrape into a serving bowl with a rubber spatula and taste for salt; you might need to add more, depending on how salty the canned beans are. Drizzle with about 1 teaspoon olive oil and serve it with the crostini.

> That's the basic recipe and you can leave it just like that. Or you can mess with it: Before adding the oil, stir in chopped parsley or basil, or sprinkle the top with ground cumin or paprika and/or either of the herbs, or scatter some tomatoes over the top.

green olive tapenade

MAKES ABOUT 1 CUP

1 pint (about 1/2 pound) large green olives, pitted, but not stuffed (see Note)
1 medium garlic clove
2 teaspoons drained, rinsed capers
1 teaspoon anchovy paste
Grated zest of 1 lemon
Grated zest of 1 orange (optional)
5 tablespoons extra-virgin olive oil

> Combine everything in the food processor and process to a rough paste.

NOTE: Pitted, unstuffed olives are often available at supermarket delis. But olives sold *with* the pits are likely to be fresher and hence of better quality. To pit, place the olives on a cutting board and roll a rolling pin over to crush them; it's very easy then to pull open each olive individually and pop out the pit.

roasted garlic

If you've never had roasted garlic, you have to try it. Garlic becomes much mellower and sweeter when it's been roasted.

MAKES 1 HEAD

1 head of garlic
Extra-virgin olive oil
1/4 teaspoon kosher salt

> Preheat the oven to 400°F.

> Break apart the head of garlic into cloves (peels still on) and put in a small baking dish. Drizzle with the oil, sprinkle with the salt, and roast until tender, 25 to 30 minutes. Serve warm or at room temperature in little bowls; your guests can squeeze the soft garlic out of the skins onto the crostini. Or, if you're feeling more helpful, squeeze the garlic into little serving bowls and present them with small spreading knives.

+ *VARIATION:* Whole Roasted Garlic
Here's a great presentation alongside steaks or salads, or for bread service: *whole* heads of roasted garlic in little bowls, one head per bowl. It's the kind of thing you might see in a French bistro. Trim off the top of the garlic bulb so that you cut into the meat of the cloves 1/4 inch or so, drizzle olive oil onto the exposed garlic, and season with salt and freshly ground black pepper. Bake uncovered for 50 minutes at 400°F.

Tuna tartare that kicks

Tuna tartare is a very popular appetizer in restaurants, but it's less common (and thus more impressive) to see it prepped by a home cook. The thing is, it's really easy, and it packs fantastic flavors. You just have to be sure to start with the freshest, highest-quality, sushi-grade tuna, sourced from a really good fish place or high-quality natural market such as Whole Foods. (And keep it refrigerated.) Also, it needs to be tossed together at the last minute; if made too far ahead, the lemon juice will "cook" and toughen the fish. Prep everything beforehand; it'll only take a few minutes to get it ready when company arrives.

I like to serve this hors d'oeuvre on individual spoons; it's as easy for guests to eat it as it is for you to plate it. (This requires a collection of about 12 extra spoons in addition to your everyday flatware set — buy funky designs at vintage shops, or just borrow some from your next-door neighbor.) Fill each with a nice big bite of tuna, and arrange them on a tray that's been lined with a linen napkin.

SERVES 4 / WINE PAIRING: Ice-cold Sake, very dry Riesling, or Sancerre

2 tablespoons extra-virgin olive oil

1 teaspoon dark sesame oil

1 teaspoon soy sauce

$3/4$ teaspoon wasabi paste

1 pound sushi-quality tuna, cut into $1/4$-inch dice

3 tablespoons chopped fresh cilantro

1 scallion, green part only, finely chopped

Juice of $1/2$ lemon, or as needed

1 English cucumber (the long, skinny kind), optional

> In a medium bowl, combine the oils, soy sauce, and wasabi, and stir to dissolve the wasabi. Add the tuna, cilantro, scallion, and lemon juice, and toss gently. Taste and add a little more lemon juice if you want a sharper flavor.

> When you're ready to serve, arrange the spoons on a lined platter. Carefully fill each spoon with tartare. Refrigerate the remaining tartare. Serve immediately.

+ *VARIATION:* **Tuna Tartare Salad**
To turn this into a more substantial dish: Make a sesame-lemon vinaigrette by whisking together 2 teaspoons fresh lemon juice (from about $1/2$ small lemon), 4 teaspoons extra-virgin olive oil, $1/8$ teaspoon kosher salt, and $1/4$ teaspoon toasted sesame oil. Toss the dressing with 4 loosely packed cups of mâche or other soft lettuce. Make a bed of the dressed lettuce on each of 4 plates, spoon the tartare on top, and serve.

Edamame

Here's another effortless cocktail food. Keep a package in the freezer for last-minute guests. I've seen shelled beans in the supermarket recently; that's *not* what you want. Popping the beans out of their shells and into your mouth is half the fun.

SERVES 4

Kosher salt for boiling beans, plus $1/2$ teaspoon for seasoning
12 ounces frozen edamame (soy bean) pods

> Bring a large saucepan of well-salted water (1 teaspoon salt per quart of water) to a boil. Add the edamame and cook until the beans, when popped out of the shell, are tender but still offer a lot of resistance when you bite into them, about 5 minutes. (They're not exactly crisp, like a green bean. But they should have chew.) Drain in a colander, and toss with $1/2$ teaspoon salt in a serving bowl. Serve warm.

+ *VARIATION:* Edamame with Sesame Seeds
Toast 1 tablespoon of sesame seeds in a frying pan over medium heat until lightly browned and fragrant, 3 to 5 minutes. Shake the pan often for even browning. Add the sesame seeds to the cooked beans with the salt.

Warm blue cheese—stuffed dates with prosciutto

As these bake, the flavor of the dates fades into the background, leaving only a hint of sweetness to balance the salty cheese and ham.

SERVES ABOUT 8 PEOPLE

1 pint (about $3/4$ pound) dates, pitted
4 ounces blue cheese, at room temperature
12 thin slices prosciutto (about $1/2$ pound)
Extra-virgin olive oil, for brushing

> Preheat the oven to 350°F.

> Line a baking sheet with parchment paper.

> Cut the dates open lengthwise with a small knife (don't cut through both sides) and stuff each with about $1/2$ teaspoon of the blue cheese. Cut the prosciutto slices in half crosswise and then in half again lengthwise. (The slices won't cut perfectly into quarters; sometimes you'll need to cut them in halves or thirds.) Roll each date in a piece of prosciutto and place on the prepared baking sheet. Spear each with a toothpick and brush with a tiny bit of oil. Put the sheet in the oven and bake for 10 minutes. Arrange on a platter and serve warm.

pizza When you've got the munchies, there's nothing better than pizza. Sure, you can order in pizza any time you want. So why make it? Because you can make it however you like, because you can probably make it better than anybody else, and because making pizza is *fun,* whether you're doing it from scratch or with store-bought dough or even on lavash flatbread (or Boboli, for that matter). It's especially fun to do with a crowd. And pizza is easy if you get the crust rolled out thin, and use a pizza stone in your oven.

I had an epiphany about pizza when I moved to New York: Good pizza is really about the bread. All New York pizzerias smell fragrant and yeasty, like a bread bakery. At any given moment in New York, there are twenty-five million balls of dough rising, and they all smell great. Chicago is a deep-dish town. It's my adopted hometown, and I will always love it for Pizzeria Uno, Due, Malnati's, and Giordano's. But those guys go way overboard with the gooey factor—I mean, I love cheese, but I don't need six pounds of it on one pie. I like New York pizza because it's more like the pizza the founding fathers intended—that is, the cracker-crust pizza of Naples and Rome. They go lightly enough with cheese and other toppings that you can actually taste the bread. In fact, a simple pizza with herbs and salt, and no cheese at all, is a thing of great beauty.

Basic pizza dough

One-half package of yeast will give you a very thin, crisp crust. If you like a puffier, breadier crust, use the whole package; the rest of the ingredient quantities in the recipe stay the same. Whichever way you go, you can't lose. If you live in an area that gets very humid, you might find one day that the 3 cups of flour just doesn't do it—the dough is wet and sticky. In which case, go ahead and add a little more flour. The humidity is simply making the dough wetter. The opposite goes for those of you in Death Valley.

MAKES ENOUGH DOUGH FOR 2 SMALLISH (10- TO 12-INCH) PIZZAS

$1/2$ package active dry yeast

1 cup warm water

2 tablespoons extra-virgin olive oil, plus 1 teaspoon for greasing the bowl

3 cups all-purpose flour

2 teaspoons kosher salt

> In a large bowl, stir together the yeast, water, and 2 tablespoons oil. Then add the flour, sprinkle the salt over, and stir into the wet ingredients with a spoon. When the dough gets too stiff to stir with the spoon, knead in the unincorporated flour by hand, picking up the dough with one hand and pressing it against the sides and bottom of the bowl to pick up any bits, and then folding it over on itself so that it all sticks together. Do this until you have a coherent (if still messy) ball of dough.

> Turn out the dough onto a clean work surface and knead for 10 minutes. (If kneading is not on your top-ten list of things you love to do, 3 to 5 minutes will suffice, or get a mixer with a dough hook.) At the beginning, the dough will be sticky; but don't add flour and don't flour the work surface. (If your hands have wet dough sticking to them, wash them so that the dough doesn't stick to your hands.) Just keep kneading. The soft dough will eventually get very smooth and supple.

> Rinse the bowl, dry it, and grease it with the remaining 1 teaspoon of oil. Put the dough into the bowl; cover with plastic wrap or a kitchen towel and let rise in a warm, draft-free place until it has increased about $1/2$ times in volume, about 1 hour. (If you're not ready when the dough is, just punch it down again and let it sit until you're ready for it. It's not going anywhere.)

Pizzas "quattro stagione"

That translates to *Four Seasons Pizzas,* and I'm not talking about the hotel chain. Rather, it's about seasonal cooking, using only ingredients that are at their best for the current time of year.

By the way, don't worry about making your pizzas perfectly round—a rustic, irregular shape is more interesting and beautiful.

winter pizza with sausage, provolone, and spinach

Hale and hearty, with toppings that are delicious and available during the coldest months. Make this with any sausage you like, including lamb sausage.

MAKES 2 SMALLISH (10- TO 12-INCH) PIZZAS / WINE PAIRING: Valpolicella

$3/4$ pound sweet Italian or other fresh sausage

1 tablespoon plus 2 teaspoons extra-virgin olive oil

Cornmeal or all-purpose flour, for dusting work surface

1 recipe Basic Pizza Dough (page 37), risen to $1^{1}/_{2}$ times original volume

$1^{1}/_{2}$ cups Basic Tomato Sauce (page 66) or store-bought tomato sauce

4 ounces fresh baby spinach

6 ounces Provolone cheese, grated on the fine holes of a grater

$1/2$ cup freshly grated Pecorino-Romano cheese

2 tablespoons chopped flat-leaf parsley

> Preheat the oven to 500°F. Put a clean, dry pizza stone in the oven and heat for about 25 minutes.

> Slit the casing on the sausage and pull it off. Heat a scant tablespoon of oil in a frying pan over medium heat. Add the sausage to the pan and cook, stirring every now and then and breaking it up with a wooden spoon into bite-size pieces, until browned, about 8 minutes. Drain the sausage on paper towels and set aside.

> Dust a work surface with cornmeal or flour. Cut the pizza dough in two and put one half on the work surface; set the other half aside. Use your fingers to flatten the dough into a disk. Press and stretch the dough to make a thin circle or rectangle, 10 to 12 inches in diameter and $1/4$ inch thick.

> If you have a pizza paddle, sprinkle it with cornmeal or flour and transfer the dough round to the paddle. If you don't have a pizza paddle, use a large cutting board or rimless baking sheet. Coat the dough with half of the tomato sauce. Sprinkle with half of the sausage. Add a couple handfuls of spinach leaves, then sprinkle the whole thing with half of the Provolone. Drizzle with 2 teaspoons olive oil. Open the oven door, pull out the rack, and put the dough round directly on the pizza stone.

> Close the oven door and turn the heat down to 475°F. Bake until the edges of the pizza are lightly browned, 12 to 15 minutes. Remove from the oven and sprinkle with half the Pecorino and half the parsley. Cut into wedges and serve. Repeat to make the second pizza.

spring pizza with fontina, sweet green peas, and pepperoni

My friend Kate was once fond of delivering this quote in an English accent, whenever the Chicago weather drew warmer: "It's spring! Have you taken a lover?" If you haven't, perhaps you'll find solace in a pizza. The peas are sweet, the Fontina is light, the pepperoni is salty. People with cheaper senses of humor might make a joke about love and pepperoni, but not me.

MAKES 2 SMALLISH (10- TO 12-INCH) PIZZAS / WINE PAIRING: Sicilian Nero d'Avola

Cornmeal or all-purpose flour, for dusting work surface
1 recipe Basic Pizza Dough (page 37), risen to $1\frac{1}{2}$ times original volume
$1\frac{1}{2}$ cups frozen, unthawed peas
6 ounces finely grated Fontina cheese
$\frac{1}{3}$ pound pepperoni, sliced thin
Extra-virgin olive oil, for drizzling
2 tablespoons chopped fresh basil (optional)

> Preheat the oven to 500°F. Put a clean, dry pizza stone in the oven and heat for about 45 minutes.

> Dust a work surface with cornmeal or flour. Cut the pizza dough in two and put one half on the work surface; set the other half aside. Use your fingers to flatten the dough into a disk. Press and stretch the dough to make a thin circle or rectangle, about 10 to 12 inches in diameter and $\frac{1}{4}$ inch thick.

> If you have a pizza paddle, sprinkle it with cornmeal or flour and transfer the dough round to the paddle. If you don't have a pizza paddle, use a large cutting board or rimless baking sheet. Sprinkle the dough with half of the frozen peas and then with half of the cheese. Scatter half of the pepperoni over the top. Open the oven door, pull out the rack, and put the dough round directly on the pizza stone.

> Close the oven and turn the heat down to 475°F. Bake until the edges of the pizza are lightly browned, 12 to 15 minutes. Remove the pizza from the oven and drizzle with olive oil; sprinkle with basil, if using. Cut into wedges and serve. Repeat to make the second pizza.

summer grilled pizza with mozzarella and fresh tomatoes

Grilling is the surest way I know to get a crisp crust on a pizza. The difficulty with grilled pizza is the heat of the fire: You want it hot enough to brown the underside of the crust but not so hot that it burns. Also important: Go easy with the toppings, as they'll have very little time to cook.

MAKES 2 SMALLISH (10- TO 12-INCH) PIZZAS / WINE PAIRING: Barbera

Cornmeal or all-purpose flour, for dusting work surface
1 recipe Basic Pizza Dough (page 37), risen to $1^1/_2$ times original volume
$^1/_2$ to $^3/_4$ pound fresh mozzarella
1 pound ripe tomatoes
$^1/_4$ cup torn fresh basil leaves
1 teaspoon coarse sea salt or kosher salt
$^1/_4$ cup plus 4 teaspoons extra-virgin olive oil
2 teaspoons red wine or balsamic vinegar (optional)

> Build a fire in your grill or preheat a gas grill.

> Sprinkle a work surface with cornmeal or lightly flour it. Cut the pizza dough in two and set one half on the work surface; set the other aside. Flatten with your fingertips to a disk. Gradually pull the dough out from the center to stretch it into whatever shape you like, about 10 to 12 inches in diameter and $^1/_4$ inch thick. Put the dough round on a cookie sheet and cover with a piece of plastic wrap. Repeat with the second dough ball and stack it on top of the first. Put the cookie sheet in the refrigerator so the dough firms up a bit.

> Now check the grill. You want a medium fire, so that the dough can cook for 2 to 3 minutes without burning. Hold your hand about 5 inches above the fire; if you can hold it there for 3 to 4 seconds, your fire is the right heat. If it's too hot, let it burn down a bit more or, if using gas, turn down to medium or medium-low.

> Meanwhile, cut the mozzarella into thin slices. Core and slice the tomatoes. Gather the mozzarella, tomatoes, basil, and salt together next to the grill. Pour about $^1/_4$ cup of oil into a bowl and put that next to the grill along with a pastry brush.

> Brush the top round of dough all over with oil. Pick it up, overturn it onto one hand, then place it oiled side down on the grill. (Return the second round to the refrigerator.) Cook the crust for 2 to 3 minutes, until the dough bubbles on the top and is cooked on the bottom. Use a pair of tongs to check it every now and then and make sure it is not burning. Use the tongs to turn the crust. Now arrange half of the cheese over the crust. Arrange half the tomato slices on top. Cover and cook until the cheese melts, 2 to 3 more minutes.

> Use 2 pairs of tongs or a metal spatula to remove the pizza to a cutting board. Sprinkle with about $^1/_2$ teaspoon salt, drizzle with 2 teaspoons olive oil, and scatter half of the basil over the top. Drizzle with 1 teaspoon vinegar, if you like. Serve immediately. Prepare and cook the second pizza in the same way.

autumn pizza with mushrooms, figs, pecorino, and duck

My childhood best friend, Ted Seifert, and his wife Nancy were the first peers of mine ever to get seriously into food. They served me crostini with goat cheese and fresh dill, then an individual beef Wellington, when we were all still in college; it was an eye-opener. Decades later, when Ted was working with a wine distributor in Bellingham, Washington, he took me to a winemaker dinner with Joel Peterson of the excellent Ravenswood winery (famous for their zinfandels and for their motto, "No Wimpy Wines!"). The chef made a pizza with figs, pheasant, and rosemary. I've modified it a bit with duck confit, because it's a little easier to find than pheasant. Prosciutto or even a good southern ham like a Smithfield will also give a perfect, salty counterpoint to the sweet figs.

MAKES 2 SMALLISH (10- TO 12-INCH) PIZZAS / WINE PAIRING: Light Chianti

1 duck confit leg, or 3 slices prosciutto or thin-sliced ham, torn into pieces
2 tablespoons plus 4 teaspoons extra-virgin olive oil
2 garlic cloves, smashed
1 pound assorted wild mushrooms
1/4 teaspoon kosher salt
1/4 teaspoon freshly ground black pepper
1/4 cup chopped flat-leaf parsley
Cornmeal or all-purpose flour, for dusting
1 recipe Basic Pizza Dough (page 37), risen to 1 1/2 times original volume
2 small balls (about 1/2 pound) fresh mozzarella, cut into thin slices
4 Mission figs, cut into small pieces
Several thin slices of red onion
Freshly grated Pecorino

> If using confit, preheat the oven to 350°F.

> Put the confit into a small frying pan over medium heat, skin side down, and brown for 3 to 5 minutes. Then transfer to the oven and bake until warmed through, about 15 minutes. Remove from the oven and let cool. When cool, skin, bone, and cut into bite-size pieces.

> Raise the oven heat to 500°F. and place a clean, dry pizza stone in the oven for about 25 minutes.

> Meanwhile, heat 2 tablespoons of olive oil in a large frying pan over a medium flame. Add the garlic and cook slowly to flavor the oil, about 5 minutes. Turn the heat to medium high, add the mushrooms, and cook, stirring every now and then, until lightly browned, about 5 minutes. Sprinkle with salt and pepper, and half of the parsley. Stir in the duck.

> Dust a work surface with cornmeal or flour. Cut the pizza dough in two and put half on the work surface; set the other half aside. Use your fingers to flatten the dough into a disk. Press and stretch the dough to make a $\frac{1}{4}$-inch-thick rectangle or circle, about 12 inches in diameter.

> If you have a pizza paddle, sprinkle it with cornmeal or flour and transfer the dough to the paddle. If you don't have a pizza paddle, use a large cutting board or rimless baking sheet. Cover the dough round with half of the mushroom—duck mixture (if using prosciutto instead of duck, lay half that atop the mushrooms) then half of the mozzarella slices and half of the fig pieces. Scatter some of the onion slices over the top. Drizzle with 2 teaspoons of olive oil. Open the oven door, pull out the rack, and put the dough round directly on the pizza stone.

> Close the oven and turn the heat down to 475°F. Bake until the crust is crisp and lightly browned, 10 to 15 minutes. Remove from the oven with the paddle or a couple of spatulas. Put the pizza on a cutting board and sprinkle with another quarter of the parsley and some Pecorino. Cut it into pieces and serve immediately. Repeat to make the second pizza.

✳ On cheeses and pizza

You can use many different cheeses on pizza. I adore fresh mozzarella, but I use the packaged stuff too. Both have merit. The texture of fresh is so great when it melts—it's smooth and light, with a pleasing tooth-someness. The other stuff is fun because when you bite into it, it has that great, stringy ropiness. Use blue cheese sparingly, because it's strong. Pecorino's delicious; Parmigiano, of course; even soft, rich cheeses like Camembert work, but put them on about halfway through the cooking so that they don't melt away into oily nothingness. One way to think about cheeses is that you want a combination of a melting cheese, like a mozzarella or Fontina, that provides a base and texture; and a dry, grating cheese such as Pecorino, that you grate over the pizza after it comes out of the oven, and that acts as a seasoning.

For best results, you need a pizza stone (because it wicks moisture out of the dough and thus makes it crispy) and a wooden paddle or a nonstick baking sheet with no edge, so you can build the pie and slide it onto the piping-hot stone.

happy hour: five classic cocktails, and five originals

Cocktails are like fashion: it's fun to adopt a new drink every so often, just as you do a new look. But, then, there are the classics — drinks that are more about enduring style than fleeting trends. To be a good host, **it helps to have a working knowledge of the latest** *and* **the greatest,** and to become conversant enough with both to occasionally innovate behind the bar. This is a good start. You want to **have a decent selection of glassware, essential tools** (shaker, jigger, strainer, etc.), and you need to **stock up on garnishes.** It's just not a gin and tonic without the lime. You also want to use the highest quality ingredients, always, from top-shelf liquors to freshly squeezed juices. Your drinks, just as your cooking, can only be as good as the stuff that goes into them.

Of course, no introduction to mixology could be complete without the martini, the silver bullet, the pinnacle of happy hour elegance. I'm not talking about desecrations like the so-called chocolate martini, or the apple-tini, or anything else silly or sugary. I'm talking about the real thing. I like to taste the vermouth in my martini; I want it dry, but not ridiculously so (if you want straight gin, you can drink it out of the bottle, ya know?). You can also make something approximating a martini with vodka, which I'll admit is far more popular than gin, and has been favored by such estimable figures as James Bond. And speaking of Bond, you can prepare the drink either shaken or stirred; either way produces delicious results, although the shaker is more festive.

By the way, don't store your martini ingredients in the freezer; room-temperature liquor will melt just the right amount of ice in the shaker or pitcher to keep your drink at the correct octane. Also, always chill your cocktail glasses by filling them with ice water before serving, and then shaking them dry before you pour.

the cosmopolitan

The fad drink of the nineties has cemented itself as a classic — it's refreshing, it's fruity without being overly sweet, it's a great balance of flavors and aromas. For variety, try it with raspberry or citrus vodka. For a more butch version — which is to say, one that isn't pink — try white grape juice instead of cranberry, and add more lime. Here's another tip: When you're ordering one of these in a really crowded bar, have the bartender put it in a rocks glass instead of a martini glass, and you won't end up with half the drink on your shoes.

1 ounce vodka
½ ounce Cointreau
½ ounce fresh lime juice
½ ounce cranberry juice
Lime wedge or twist of orange peel, for garnish

> Shake all ingredients except garnish in a shaker half filled with ice until very cold; strain into a chilled cocktail glass. Garnish with lime wedge on the rim, and serve.

red hot

For boys with too much macho for Cosmopolitans, or something else to prove. This also works with any white spirit, such as gin, blanco tequila, or white rum.

2 ounces vodka
½ ounce Campari
4 or 5 — or 6 or 7 — dashes of Tabasco sauce
Red Hots, for garnish

> Shake over ice and serve straight up in a chilled cocktail glass. Garnish with a couple of Red Hots dropped into the bottom.

the greyhound

This is such a simple drink you barely need a recipe. But apart from the fact that I love it, I include it here because it illustrates the correct proportions of liquor-to-mixer for virtually any highball. Use these same measures for a gin and tonic, a vodka and soda, a rum and Coke; done. For variations, try ruby-red grapefruit juice or fruit-infused vodka.

2 ounces vodka
5 ounces grapefruit juice
½ orange slice, if you like, for garnish

> Pour the vodka and grapefruit juice into a highball glass filled with ice, and stir well until chilled. Serve with orange slice on the rim.

the classic martini

This is the cocktail in its purest form, clean, clear, and astringent. Because of that, you have to use the best quality ingredients. I like Noilly Prat dry vermouth with gin, such as Bombay Sapphire, Tanquerey, or, for a twist, the curiously cucumber-y Hendrickson. Want to be really classy? Spear the olives on sterling silver picks; you can find great vintage barware like these in antique stores.

$1\frac{1}{2}$ ounces best-quality gin
$\frac{1}{2}$ ounce dry vermouth
Green olives

> Shake or stir the ingredients with ice until it's shockingly, blisteringly cold, at least 10 seconds (or until you can barely stand holding the shaker). Strain into a cocktail glass and garnish with 1 to 3 olives.

+ *VARIATION:* **Dirty Martini**
For a dirty martini, splash a little olive juice into the glass.

the really, really bloody mary

The all-star bevvie of brunch—or for the morning after too many martinis. This cocktail is practically a salad, especially when you make it with the multi-veggie V-8 juice instead of ordinary tomato juice. Warning: I like it really spicy, with a triple-whammy of freshly ground black pepper, Tabasco sauce, and ground horseradish. Or make it a quadruple with a little dollop of wasabi paste—clears the sinuses and gets the endorphins going.

2 ounces vodka (I like Absolut, Ketel One, or—yep—Smirnoff)
4 ounces V-8 vegetable juice
Juice of $\frac{1}{2}$ lime
$1\frac{1}{2}$ teaspoons Worcestershire sauce
$1\frac{1}{2}$ teaspoons ground horseradish
4 dashes Tabasco sauce
Celery salt to taste
Freshly ground black pepper to taste
Lime wedge, for garnish
Spear of blanched asparagus or celery stalk, for garnish

> Shake all ingredients except the lime and asparagus in a shaker half full of ice until very cold; strain into a chilled highball glass. Garnish with the lime and celery and serve.

the margarita

Here's one that's been bastardized 800 ways from Sunday. For me, it's never better than when made the classic way: on the rocks with salt. Works best with coarse salt milled for margarita-making in mind; you can buy the stuff in containers ready-made to have your glass dipped in. Don't use the $50-a-bottle añejo sipping tequila for this—the subtleties will be lost under the barrage of sweetness and lime. Having a party? Multiply the recipe several times and put it in pitchers.

Lime wedges
Margarita salt, or other coarse salt such as kosher salt
1½ ounces tequila
½ ounce Cointreau (preferably) or Triple Sec
1 ounce fresh lime juice

> Run the rim of the glass with a wedge of lime to moisten it, then dip the glass in the salt. Shake the tequila, Cointreau, and lime juice in a shaker half filled with ice, and strain into a glass. Garnish with a lime wedge on the rim.

the steadfast

You might call this an Italian take on the old-fashioned, if the Italian had stopped off in New Orleans on the way to Kentucky. Created by my great friend and raconteur Terry Sullivan for his wife, the Steadfast Monica, to sip at the end of a long day trying to teach English to thirteen-year-olds.

For a light version, I recommend Basil Hayden's, Jim Beam's gentlest small-batch bourbon, which Terry considers a Ladies' Whiskey. On the other hand, for the end of a particularly long day, try their 125-plus proof Booker's.

2 ounces bourbon
1 ounce maraschino (clear, sweet, cherry liqueur that is widely available but underappreciated)
4 or 5 good dashes of Peychaud's bitters (from New Orleans, the secret ingredient in the Sazerac, available at any good spirits dealer; adds a lovely red color)
Orange twist or cherry, for garnish

> Build the drink over ice in a double old-fashioned glass, stir, and garnish with an orange twist or cherry.

the brazilian

Not to be confused with the bikini-waxing style. If Hemingway had gone to Rio, and been a touch more (or less) sure of his sexuality, he might have slurped these. Or something.

2 ounces of Cachaça (the famous Brazilian spirit, made with sugarcane)
2 ounces grapefruit juice
1/2 ounce simple syrup (see Notes)
1 egg white (see Notes)
Grapefruit zest, for garnish

> In a blender, blend all ingredients with 1/2 cup of shaved ice. Serve in a stemmed glass, garnished with a curl of grapefruit zest.

NOTES: *Simple Syrup:* Combine equal portions of sugar and water in a saucepan over low heat and cook until the sugar melts. Chill before using.

Egg whites: It's yolks that are the bad guys. Whites are great for adding body to a drink. They are also much less likely than yolks to carry salmonella.

amalfi tonic

An Amalfi Coast take on the gin and tonic. You could also use vodka.

2 ounces gin
1 ounce limoncello
5 ounces tonic
Lemon twist, for garnish

> Mix the gin and limoncello over ice, top with tonic, and garnish with a lemon twist.

the garnet

Here's the thing: This one doesn't have any alcohol in it. Why? Because your first and foremost responsibility as a host is to make all your guests feel welcome and happy, and most of us have friends who don't drink—or, at a minimum, who don't *always* drink. These friends deserve just as interesting and fresh a beverage as the boozers.

2 sprigs mint
2 ounces pomegranate juice
1 cube frozen orange juice
6 ounces Perrier sparkling water

> Crush 1 mint sprig in the bottom of a rocks glass. Add the pomegranate juice and the orange-juice cube. Top with Perrier and garnish with the other sprig of mint.

2 / Graze: salads, green and otherwise

The problem with salads, if there is one, is dressings. It's easier than ever to get great vegetables these days, with so many stores emphasizing organic and regionally grown produce (see "What *Is* Organic Food?" page 53), and with farmers' markets in every community. But virtually every salad dressing on the grocery shelf is depressing, at best, if not downright awful, filled with weird thickeners and sweeteners and tons of preservatives. (One of the very few exceptions is Newman's Own balsamic vinaigrette.)

The good news: Making fresh salad dressings at home is really easy, and they're infinitely better. It takes only minutes to make an actual vinaigrette — that is, a recipe for which you measure out ingredients, including vinegar, and whisk them together in a bowl to emulsify — to dress your salad. But you can also just drizzle some oil and vinegar or lemon juice over a bowl of greens, season with salt and pepper, and call it a day. Done.

I've given you several salad recipes here that use vinaigrettes and particular combinations of ingredients that taste good with them. But what you really need to throw a salad together is simple ratios: so much vinegar or lemon juice to so much oil. An all-around standard ratio is one part vinegar (or citrus juice) to three parts oil. Start with a little bit of dressing and keep adding if it's not enough; nobody likes a soggy salad.

✷ Oil for salads

The oil must have a strong enough taste to balance the acid in the vinegar. I wouldn't recommend making a vinaigrette with a bland variety such as canola or vegetable oil; they just don't have enough flavor, so the dressing tastes too vinegary and harsh. Peanut oil has a little more character (that's what they use in France when they don't want the rich, fruity taste of olive oil). There also are a wealth of flavored oils and vinegars — yes, those tall bottles stuffed with seeds, garlic cloves, and plant branches aren't just for decorating the kitchen. Try them out using the ratios above. For example, the O Olive Oil Company from San Rafael makes a great organic olive oil infused with ruby grapefruit that pairs beautifully with champagne vinegar on a salad alongside light fare like grilled fish or chicken.

Basic vinaigrettes

Here are a few simple vinaigrettes to get you going. They are easily doubled in case you want to make a large batch and stick it in the refrigerator for the week. (I wouldn't recommend this for the citrus vinaigrette, since the citrus gets old within a couple of days.)

mustardy vinaigrette

MAKES ABOUT 3/4 CUP

2 teaspoons Dijon mustard
2 tablespoons red or white wine vinegar
1/4 teaspoon kosher salt
1/4 teaspoon freshly ground black pepper
1/2 cup extra-virgin olive oil
1 small shallot, chopped

> In a small bowl, use a whisk to blend together the mustard with the vinegar, salt, and pepper. Then, while whisking quickly, slowly drizzle in the olive oil so that the oil and watery ingredients mix together. If you add the oil slowly enough, they will emulsify and *stay* mixed together. Add the shallot.

> Even easier: If you don't mind shaking the dressing each time before pouring it, don't bother emulsifying. Just put all the ingredients in a jar with a lid, close the lid, and shake well to combine.

balsamic vinaigrette

MAKES ABOUT 1/2 CUP

1 teaspoon Dijon mustard
2 tablespoons balsamic vinegar
1/4 teaspoon kosher salt
1/4 teaspoon freshly ground black pepper
1 small garlic clove, chopped
1/3 cup extra-virgin olive oil

> In a small bowl, whisk the mustard with the vinegar, salt, pepper, and garlic. Slowly add the olive oil. Or just put all the ingredients in a jar with a lid, close the lid, and shake well to combine.

citrus vinaigrette

Tastes good with a mixture of chopped fresh herbs such as basil, tarragon, cilantro, and parsley.

MAKES ABOUT $\frac{1}{2}$ CUP

3 tablespoons fresh orange juice (from about 1 medium juicing orange)
1 tablespoon fresh lemon juice (from about $\frac{1}{2}$ lemon)
$\frac{1}{8}$ teaspoon kosher salt
$\frac{1}{8}$ teaspoon freshly ground black pepper
$\frac{1}{4}$ cup extra-virgin olive oil
4 medium basil leaves, folded in half lengthwise and cut crosswise into
   thin slivers

> In a small bowl, whisk the orange and lemon juices with the salt and pepper. Slowly whisk in the olive oil and then the basil. Or put all of the ingredients in a jar with a lid, close the lid, and shake well to combine.

✳ What *is* organic food?

Here's what it's not: It's not about a meatless diet, bland flavors, hippies, or food with bugs in it. (Well, okay, it *is* about hippies—but not *only* hippies.)

Organic food is better. Period. It just means food (and animals we consume as food) that is raised naturally—that is, without weird growth-inducing hormones, antibiotics, pesticides, colors, waxes, or anything else likely to give you a horrible disease some-day. It's meat from cows that are fed only grain and grass, not ground meat by-products (which are thought to be a cause of mad cow disease). It sometimes means food that doesn't look as perfect under the bright lights in the grocery store, but that ninety-nine percent of the time tastes better. It is, in short, food raised the old-fashioned way. Because of that, it's slightly more expensive (and sometimes much *more* than slightly: I once carried an organic honeydew melon to the checkout counter in a Chicago store, and thought better of it when the damned thing rang up at twelve bucks), but for the most part, it's worth it.

Mesclun salad with pears, blue cheese, and walnuts

Walnut oil has a rich, warm taste that brings out the sweetness in a ripe pear. But it's also a bit of a gourmet item. If you don't feel like running out to buy it, that's fine—the salad works well with just olive oil, too. Try it in springtime with arugula, when that peppery green is at its best, instead of the mesclun.

SERVES 4 / WINE PAIRING: Rich Trebbiano or Champagne

2 teaspoons unsalted butter

1/4 cup walnut pieces

8 cups mesclun or arugula

1 tablespoon balsamic vinegar

2 tablespoons walnut oil

1 tablespoon extra-virgin olive oil

1/8 teaspoon kosher salt

1/8 teaspoon freshly ground black pepper

1 ripe pear such as Bartlett or Comice, cored and sliced

2 ounces excellent-quality blue cheese

> In a small frying pan, melt the butter over a medium flame. Add the walnuts and let them cook, shaking the pan occasionally, until they begin to brown, 3 to 4 minutes. Take the pan off the heat and let cool.

> Put the lettuces in a large bowl. Add the vinegar, oils, salt, and pepper, and toss gently. Taste to see if the salad needs more salt or pepper. Divide the mixture among 4 plates. Arrange the pear slices over the greens, sprinkle with the toasted walnuts, and crumble the cheese over (or cut the cheese into slices and arrange on top of the lettuces). Serve immediately.

✳ Shelf life

A word of warning: Oils and vinegars spoil if they sit around too long. Oil gets rancid—toasted oils especially. Sesame and nut oils should be kept in the refrigerator. Other oils will turn rancid very slowly at room temperature (a question of months); if you use them often, you should use them up before you have a problem. But if you use them rarely, you may find that you need to throw out an old oil and replace it. Vinegars will get strong and harsh-tasting as they get old, but I'm talking about several years. You can keep freshly squeezed lemon juice overnight in the fridge but that's it; the taste starts to change after that.

Spicy asian slaw with sesame and sweet red pepper

I love cole slaw; it's an easy, durable salad that can withstand being predressed for as many as two days because cabbage is so sturdy. There are two basic kinds of slaws: those made with a creamy, mayonnaise-style base, and those made with a vinaigrette. This is an Asian-style vinaigrette. For added color, use half green cabbage and half purple.

SERVES 6 TO 8 / WINE PAIRING: Fruity Beaujolais or New Zealand Sauvignon Blanc

2 tablespoons rice vinegar or white wine vinegar
Juice of 1 lime (about 1 tablespoon)
$1/2$ teaspoon soy sauce
$1/2$ teaspoon kosher salt
$1/8$ teaspoon freshly ground black pepper
$1/2$ teaspoon sugar
$1/4$ cup peanut oil
1 tablespoon toasted sesame oil
8 cups cored, shredded cabbage, preferably Savoy ($1/2$ medium head,
    or about 1 pound)
1 red bell pepper, cored, seeded, and slivered
1 jalapeño pepper, cored, seeded, and slivered (optional)
2 scallions, sliced
$1/2$ cup roughly chopped fresh cilantro, tender stems and leaves
2 tablespoons sesame seeds, with hull (see Note, page 101)

> In a large bowl, whisk together the vinegar, lime juice, soy sauce, salt, pepper, sugar, and oils. Add the cabbage, peppers, scallions, and cilantro, and toss.

> Toast the sesame seeds in a dry frying pan over medium heat until lightly browned and fragrant, about 5 minutes. Sprinkle the seeds over the top of the slaw and serve.

Old-school caesar salad

I love a great Caesar salad—especially when it's prepared tableside on a rolling cart. The most noble of all lettuce salads, it was named not for the Roman emperor with the George Clooney haircut, but for Caesar Cardini, the chef who created it in Tijuana, Mexico, in the 1920s. Unfortunately, what with people's hysteria about eggs and their amusing preference for Caesars with no anchovies, it's hard to find a good one.

The original featured whole leaves of romaine hearts so it could be served as finger food. (Really.) But I suggest tearing the lettuce and providing forks.

SERVES 4 / WINE PAIRING: Earthy Pinot Noir or Spanish Tempranillo

for the croutons

2 cups 1-inch bread cubes
1 tablespoon extra-virgin olive oil
1 medium garlic clove, smashed
Pinch of kosher salt
$1/8$ teaspoon freshly ground black pepper

for the dressing and salad

$1/2$ medium garlic clove
$1/2$ teaspoon kosher salt
4 to 6 fresh anchovy fillets, mashed with a fork, or 1 tablespoon anchovy paste
1 large egg
Juice of $1/2$ lemon (about 1 tablespoon)
$1/2$ teaspoon Worcestershire sauce
7 tablespoons best-quality extra-virgin olive oil
8 cups torn hearts of romaine lettuce (just the inner white leaves)
$1/3$ cup freshly grated Parmigiano-Reggiano, plus more for passing at table
$1/4$ teaspoon freshly ground black pepper

> Preheat the oven to 400°F.

> Put the bread cubes in a large bowl, drizzle with the olive oil, and toss. Then spread them out on a baking sheet and bake until golden brown and crisp, about 10 minutes. Put them back in the bowl with the garlic, salt, and pepper, and toss.

> Meanwhile, bring a saucepan of water to a boil. In a salad bowl or on a cutting board, mash the garlic and $1/2$ teaspoon salt with a fork. Mash in the anchovy fillets. When the water comes to a boil, add the egg in its shell and cook for 1 minute. Drain and cool under cold running water. Then crack into the bowl with the garlic-salt mixture (use a spoon to scrape the egg out of the shell) and whisk with a fork or whisk. Whisk in the lemon juice and Worcestershire sauce. Then gradually whisk in the olive oil.

> Add the lettuce to the bowl along with the Parmigiano, croutons, and $1/4$ teaspoon pepper. Toss, and serve immediately.

Warm spinach salad with bacon and figs

Sweet, soft ripe figs add a twist to this classic French salad, traditionally made with the hot bacon fat (yeah, baby!). I've lightened the recipe by using olive oil, but bacon fat tastes great, too. If you do opt to use the fat, get everyone to sit at the table before you start the salad. You want to serve it immediately, when the bacon fat is still hot and liquid.

The bacon can be sautéed ahead of time; remove it from the pan and discard the bacon fat. When you're ready to eat, combine the bacon and the olive oil in the pan and reheat. Dump both over the spinach in the bowl. Then continue on with the recipe. Try to get thick-sliced bacon—a solid ¼ inch thick—so it cooks into thick *lardons*, as the French call them, not skinny little bacon bits (you could ask a butcher, or at the meat counter of a good market). For a slightly more exotic taste, use sherry or a garlic-flavored vinegar instead of red wine.

SERVES 4 / WINE PAIRING: Alsatian Riesling

8 cups stemmed spinach (baby or standard) leaves, about 10 ounces
6 ounces thick-sliced (¼-inch-thick) slab bacon (about 4 slices), cut crosswise
    into ¼-inch strips
1 medium shallot, chopped (about 2 tablespoons)
3 tablespoons red wine vinegar
1 tablespoon Dijon mustard
¼ cup extra-virgin olive oil
⅛ teaspoon kosher salt
¼ teaspoon freshly ground black pepper
4 ripe Mission figs, quartered

> Put the spinach in a large salad bowl.

> Put the bacon in a medium frying pan and cook over medium heat until the fat is rendered and the bacon is well browned, about 10 minutes. Halfway through the cooking, drain off the bacon fat. When the bacon is cooked, remove it from the pan with a slotted spoon and dump it into the bowl with the spinach. Pour off the bacon fat, leaving the brown bits behind in the pan. (There'll be a bit of bacon fat left in the pan, too.)

> Add the shallot and vinegar to the pan, put it back over medium heat, and stir with a wooden spoon to pick up all the bits stuck to the bottom of the pan. Simmer until the vinegar reduces by about half, about 30 seconds. Remove the pan from the heat and whisk in the mustard. Slowly whisk in the olive oil. Use a rubber spatula to scrape the mixture into the bowl with the spinach, add the salt and pepper, and toss. Add the figs and toss very gently. Divide the warm salad among 4 plates and serve immediately.

Everything's gone greens

Very soft lettuces such as mesclun should be lightly dressed, without emulsified dressing, because they get drowned and limp very easily. Sturdier lettuces such as romaine, frisée, radicchio, arugula, spinach, Boston, and Bibb lettuces can stand up to a thicker, even a warm dressing. A newer entry to American super-market shelves is mâche (pronounced "mosh"), or lamb's leaf lettuce, a soft, mild lettuce that grows in little clumps of leaves. Various combinations of the above also are available everywhere prewashed, cut, bagged, and ready to eat. This is great news for people in a hurry, although you should always check the sell-by date for freshness and look closely through the plastic to make sure the leaves aren't turning brown at the edges, or, worse, rotting. I also find these prebagged greens slightly drier, less crispy, and less fresh tasting than head lettuce I've cleaned immediately before serving, so if you have time, do the labor yourself.

Fennel salad with shrimp and orange

Fennel has a mild licorice taste that goes well with orange. Use the best olive oil and kalamata olives you can find. This vinaigrette is also delicious with a green salad garnished with another fruit, such as sliced nectarines, peaches, or grapes, or as a sauce for fish. You can also substitute sautéed scallops for the shrimp, if you like.

SERVES 4 / WINE PAIRING: Verdicchio

for the salad

1 medium fennel bulb

1 navel orange

$1/2$ teaspoon kosher salt

$1/4$ teaspoon freshly ground black pepper

1 pound medium shrimp (20 to 24 count; see page 60), peeled and deveined

2 tablespoons extra-virgin olive oil

for the orange vinaigrette

1 navel orange

1 teaspoon red wine vinegar

$1/8$ teaspoon kosher salt

$1/8$ teaspoon freshly ground black pepper

$1/4$ cup extra-virgin olive oil

for serving

$1/4$ medium red onion, thinly sliced

4 cups arugula, washed and spun dry

2 tablespoons chopped flat-leaf parsley

$1/8$ teaspoon freshly ground black pepper

$1/2$ cup pitted kalamata olives

> Trim the stalks from the fennel bulb, if there are any, and trim the fat end as well. Cut the bulb in half and slice lengthwise as thin as possible; set aside. Peel the orange and cut crosswise into thin slices, then cut each slice in half; set the orange slices aside separately.

> In a small bowl, stir together $1/4$ teaspoon of the salt and the $1/4$ teaspoon of pepper. Lay the shrimp out in a single layer on a piece of wax or parchment paper and sprinkle with half of the seasoning mixture.

> Heat the olive oil in a large frying pan over a medium-high flame. When the oil is smoking, add the shrimp, seasoned side down in a single layer, and sprinkle with the remaining seasoning mixture. Cook for 2 minutes, until lightly browned and pink. Turn the shrimp with tongs and cook for 1 more minute. Remove to a plate, leaving the oil in the pan.

RECIPE CONTINUES

> Now add the sliced fennel to the pan, turn the heat down to medium, and sprinkle with the remaining $1/4$ teaspoon of salt. Cook, stirring, until the fennel starts to wilt, 2 to 3 minutes. Dump the fennel into a large serving bowl and let cool.

> Meanwhile, make the vinaigrette: Grate $1/2$ teaspoon zest from the orange and squeeze 3 tablespoons of the juice. Combine the juice and zest in a small bowl. Add the vinegar, $1/8$ teaspoon salt, and $1/8$ teaspoon pepper. Slowly whisk in the olive oil to emulsify.

> When the fennel has cooled to room temperature, add the cooked shrimp along with the red onion, arugula, parsley, and reserved orange slices. Pour over the dressing and toss to coat. Season with $1/8$ teaspoon pepper. Divide the mixture, excluding the shrimp, among 4 serving plates or arrange on a large platter. Scatter the shrimp and olives over the top and serve.

✳ Buying shrimp by "count"

You probably have noticed that shrimp is sold by size — that is, small, medium, large, jumbo, and perhaps colossal — and that the larger the size, the more expensive the shrimp. You've probably also noticed that these sizes are hardly ever consistent from one market to the next; one fishmonger's medium shrimp is another's large.

In the seafood industry, however, there are regulations concerning such matters, and shrimp is graded for sale by the number of shrimp to the pound. For example: 16/20 count means 16 to 20 individual shrimp of that size make up one pound; 21/25 count means 21 to 25 shrimp of that size are equal to one pound, and so on. U10s (meaning "under 10s") are very large shrimp; there are less than 10 to the pound. (U10s are often sold as "prawns" although some fish stores amuse themselves by selling 16/20s as prawns as well.)

For the purposes of these recipes, when I call for medium shrimp, I'm assuming you'll be buying shrimp that are in the range of 20 to 30 to the pound. When I call for large shrimp, I'm assuming 16 to 20 to the pound. Sometimes you'll find the count marked at the counter. If not, ask.

Panzanella

This recipe is only for tomato season. In most of the United States, that means August, September, and October, when we have the freshest, sweetest fruits of the year. With great tomatoes, especially with a blend of heirloom varieties, this salad is virtually intoxicating.

I first tasted this Italian classic over lunch with my first *Esquire* editor, Scott Omelianuk, and the magazine's then fashion director Stefano Tonchi—both great foodies and style kings—at the late, lamented Manhattan restaurant JUdson Grill. I asked chef Bill Telepan for his recipe, which used wax beans and was topped with sautéed skate wing, and it became a highlight for me every tomato season.

In my version, basil oil infuses the bread with the taste of sweet herb, garlic, and olive oil. It's a brilliant green color when you first add it to the salad but it loses its color quickly; so take the salad to the table with the oil just drizzled over the top and toss it there. If you have olive or rosemary bread, use 'em.

This salad is best served no more than 10 to 15 minutes after you put it together; any longer than that and the flavors begin to lose their crispness, and the bread becomes too soggy. The recipe for the basil oil makes more than you need; use the remainder as a sauce for fish or steak, or in place of plain oil in a vinaigrette for a green salad. Serve the salad with a couple of your favorite cheeses and it will be enough for lunch or a light dinner.

SERVES 6 TO 8 / WINE PAIRING: Dry Prosecco

2 pounds perfectly ripe tomatoes, preferably a mix of varieties and colors
    (red, yellow, orange, heirloom, etc.)
1 medium zucchini, cut into $1/2$-inch cubes
$1/2$ teaspoon kosher salt
1 pound crusty, hearty bread
2 tablespoons red wine vinegar
$1/2$ teaspoon freshly ground black pepper
$1/2$ cup Basil Oil (page 103)

> Cut the tomatoes into bite-size wedges, and place in a large bowl. Add the zucchini, sprinkle with the salt, and let stand while you prepare the rest of the salad. The salt will soften the zucchini and draw liquid out of the tomatoes, making a delicious, tomatoey liquid that soaks and flavors the bread.

> Cut the bread, with the crust, into $3/4$- to 1-inch cubes. Toast in a 400° oven for 10 minutes; remove and cool.

> To assemble the salad, first pat the zucchini dry on paper towels. In a large, attractive serving bowl, combine the tomatoes, zucchini, bread, vinegar, and black pepper. Toss. Drizzle the basil oil over and toss again just before serving.

> This also is great served over a bed of greens, such as arugula or mesclun mix.

3 / **Pasta, risotti, and a paella**

For some reason, the best things in the world come from Italy. The best clothes, the best-looking people, the best pistachio gelato. And, of course, pasta. Pasta and rice have taken a beating in recent years with this low-carb business. But not only do these grains feed the majority of the world every day, they're just too delicious and versatile to fall off my menu. In my world, it's all about variety and moderation.

Well, variety, anyway.

And pasta is about nothing more so than diversity. It's a testament to the humor and imagination of Italians that there are so many shapes being invented all the time, as limitless as the number of great cooks and vowel-packed names. Traditionally, long skinny noodles go with smoother sauces, in dishes such as pasta with olive oil, spaghetti with tomato sauce, and angel hair with cream sauce and scallops; the other shapes are good for sauces that contain little bits that get caught in the ins-and-outs of the noodles. The different shapes—penne, farfalle, cavatappi, cavatelli, orechiette—each have different abilities to cling to sauce. In the following recipes, I've given recommendations for which shapes go best with which sauces, in my opinion. But I also suggest that you experiment to find out what you like; the rules aren't hard and fast.

✳ A word on pasta sauces

There's a lot more to pasta sauces than the classic red stuff, although that is a noble topping, for sure. One very simple saucing agent is great-quality olive oil (as in the recipe for orecchiette, opposite), flavored with garlic and herbs if you like, and/or with chilies.

Cream is another important sauce base—not the lightest choice, I admit, but an enduringly popular one (witness fettuccine alfredo). I like just a little bit of cream in a tomato sauce, because the sweetness of the cream balances the acidity of the tomatoes, and because it thickens red sauce to a consistency that coats the pasta well (see the ziti on page 68). The addition of grated cheese will thicken the sauce further.

On the lighter side, and a bit more contemporary, stocks and broths make fantastic sauces for pasta, as in the recipe for Pasta en Brodo (page 74). Few people make their own stock, but there are some decent brands in the supermarket, particularly the organic, low-salt varieties. If you doctor them a little by cooking the stock with a bit of meat and vegetables, you get a quick, tasty broth. These sauces don't coat the pasta, but grated cheese and a little olive oil will help—and you typically use a fork *and* a spoon to eat pasta done this way.

✳ Parmesan cheese does not come from a green can

Parmigiano-Reggiano is the king of Italian cheeses: Aged, hard, and salty, it's a holy ingredient for many food lovers. You can spend good money on the best varieties in gourmet shops, but you can also buy a perfectly reasonable version of it in the cheese department of any grocery store, and it keeps for weeks. There is simply no reason to buy the dried, preserved, pregrated (and, most important, *tasteless*) stuff in the can. Ever. Pass it around the dinner table with a grater, or with a carrot peeler, which produces terrific, thick curls that are easy to spear with a fork.

Experiment with other dry cheeses suitable for grating: Asiago has an assertive taste that balances the strong taste of broccoli; aged Gouda goes well with sausage; Gorgonzola, while not a grating cheese, is lovely with cream or olive oil sauces; and ricotta can be stirred into a tomato sauce or an olive oil sauce for a little richness.

Orecchiette with broccoli, garlic, and asiago cheese

Orecchiette means "little ears" — one of my favorite pasta shapes. This is an embellishment of the standard *pasta al'olio,* which is simply pasta with garlic and oil, but I've added some broccoli so you get your veggies, too. Asiago is a little more acidic than Parmigiano-Reggiano and works very nicely with the broccoli. If you can't find it, use Parmigiano.

It's very convenient to have a pasta insert for your pot. (That's a second pot, with holes in it, that fits into the outer pot.) That way you can cook the broccoli in the pasta water and remove it easily, without having to fish around with your slotted spoon. Also, if you decide that the broccoli or the pasta needs more cooking, you can put them right back into the hot water. If you don't have a pasta insert, use a large slotted spoon.

SERVES 4 / WINE PAIRING: Vermentino or Sauvignon Blanc

Kosher salt for boiling pasta, plus $1/2$ teaspoon for seasoning
$1/2$ cup extra-virgin olive oil
3 large garlic cloves, sliced
$3/4$ pound broccoli crowns (see Note)
$3/8$ teaspoon freshly ground black pepper
1 pound dried orecchiette pasta
$3/4$ cup freshly grated Asiago cheese, or Parmigiano-Reggiano in a pinch, plus
    more for serving

> Bring a large pot of salted water (1 teaspoon salt per quart of water) to a boil for the pasta. Meanwhile, in a large sauté pan heat the olive oil with the garlic over a low flame to infuse the oil with the taste of the garlic without browning, about 5 minutes. Remove the pan from the heat.

> When the water comes to a boil, add the broccoli (preferably in a pasta insert) and cook for 1 minute. Remove the broccoli and add it to the pan with the oil; season with $1/2$ teaspoon salt and $1/8$ teaspoon pepper.

> Now add the pasta to the water and cook until tender but firm (al dente), about 10 minutes. Drain, and add to the broccoli mixture. Cook, tossing with tongs, over medium heat, to warm everything up and get the pasta coated with the oil. Sprinkle with the cheese and the remaining $1/4$ teaspoon pepper, and serve with the extra cheese on the side.

NOTE: Broccoli crowns are the top half of the broccoli heads, with the stem cut off, sold in many supermarkets. The advantage of the crowns is that you end up with lots of florets and not so many stems. If you can't find the crowns . . . no big deal. Just use regular broccoli.

Your basic pasta with red sauce

You have a lot of choices in the pantheon of jarred tomato sauces, but it really is worth it to make your own. This easy, garlicky marinara tastes like tomatoes, olive oil, and herbs, and it only takes about 30 minutes to cook—most of that unattended. That's about the time it takes to bring your pasta water to a boil and cook the noodles. You can use this sauce to dress any pasta you like; I particularly love a four-cheese ravioli or a penne.

SERVES 4 / WINE PAIRING: Primitivo

basic tomato sauce

$1/4$ cup extra-virgin olive oil

1 medium onion, chopped

3 medium garlic cloves, chopped or sliced

1 bay leaf

1 teaspoon fresh thyme leaves, or $1/2$ teaspoon dried thyme or oregano

10 fresh basil leaves, chopped

$1/2$ teaspoon kosher salt, plus more to taste

1 can (28 ounces) whole, peeled tomatoes, preferably San Marzano variety

$1/2$ teaspoon sugar

$1/8$ teaspoon freshly ground black pepper

for serving

1 pound dried pasta (penne, rigatoni, ravioli, whatever is handy), cooked and drained

$1/2$ cup freshly grated Parmigiano-Reggiano

> For the sauce, heat 2 tablespoons of the oil in a saucepan over a medium-low flame. Add the onion, garlic, bay leaf, thyme, basil, and salt and cook, covered, until the onion is soft and breaking down, 8 to 10 minutes. Add the tomatoes (crush them in your hands as you add them, or break them up with the side of a spoon in the pot) along with the juices and the sugar. Turn the heat to medium and simmer until the sauce is thickened, 15 to 20 minutes. Stir in the remaining 2 tablespoons of oil and the pepper, and taste for seasoning.

> Dump the drained pasta into a large bowl, add the sauce, and toss gently to coat the pasta with the sauce. Serve with the grated cheese.

+ *VARIATION:* Tomato Cream Sauce
Add $1/2$ cup heavy or whipping cream about halfway through the cooking.

+ *VARIATION:* **Putanesca**
Five minutes before the sauce finishes cooking, stir in 1½ tablespoons capers; ½ cup kalamata olives, pitted and chopped; and ½ teaspoon crushed red pepper flakes.

+ *VARIATION:* **Arrabbiata**
Cook the sauce as above, but add 1 teaspoon crushed red pepper flakes along with the garlic. Omit the thyme and add 8 fresh basil leaves when you add the tomatoes.

Ziti with sausage, tomato, mushrooms, and spinach

This is serious Guy Food. It makes me think of Chicago. Actually, it makes me think of the Superfans skit from *Saturday Night Live* ("Da Bears," and all that), only those guys probably would pick out the portobellos and spinach. You can use whatever sausage you like, including a hot Italian sausage or a lamb sausage. Try penne or rigatoni instead of the ziti.

One of the beauties of this recipe is that you can do the prep as you go along. Start by preparing the tomatoes and then slice the onions. While the onions cook, slice the mushrooms. While the sauce cooks, prep the spinach. I should point out that I'm trying not to use too much cream these days, but it really helps here to add body to the sauce. The pasta cooking liquid thins the cream, while the starch in it helps to bind the sauce. If you're on a health kick (ha, ha), use chicken stock instead of cream, and omit the pasta cooking liquid. Or see the chapter on salads.

SERVES 4 / WINE PAIRING: Italian Cabernet Franc or Aglianico

Kosher salt for boiling pasta, plus $1/2$ teaspoon for seasoning

$1^1/2$ pounds ripe plum tomatoes

2 tablespoons extra-virgin olive oil

$1/2$ pound sweet Italian pork sausage, removed from the casing, or other
    high-quality fresh sausage

1 large onion, sliced

1 bay leaf

$1/2$ pound portobello mushrooms, stemmed, caps halved and sliced crosswise
    $1/4$ inch thick

1 pound dried ziti

$1/2$ cup whipping cream

10 ounces fresh spinach, rinsed and drained, thick stems removed,
    leaves coarsely chopped

$1/4$ teaspoon freshly ground black pepper

1 cup finely grated aged Gouda cheese, or Parmigiano-Reggiano

> Bring a large, covered pot of salted water (about 4 teaspoons salt and 4 quarts water) to a boil over high heat.

> Cut the tomatoes in half through the equator and squeeze each half over the sink to release the seeds. Cut off the stem ends. Coarsely chop the tomatoes and set them aside.

> Heat the oil in a large frying pan over a medium flame. Add the sausage, onion, bay leaf, and $1/4$ teaspoon of the salt and cook, breaking up the sausage with the side of a spoon, until the onion is wilted and the sausage is browned, about 8 minutes. Stir several times during the cooking. Add the mushrooms and stir well to combine with the other ingredients. Cook, stirring every now and then, until the mushrooms are wilted, about 3 more minutes.

> The pasta water should have reached a boil by now. Add the ziti and stir to keep it from sticking together. Boil until tender but firm, 8 to 9 minutes.

> While the pasta cooks, add the cream, chopped tomatoes, and 1/4 teaspoon salt to the pan with the sausage mixture. Turn the heat to medium-low, cover, and cook for 5 to 7 minutes to soften the tomatoes. Add the spinach and 1/4 cup of the pasta cooking water. Cover and cook for 3 more minutes to wilt the spinach; stir once during the cooking. Remove the bay leaf.

> When the pasta is cooked, drain it in a colander, reserving about 1/4 cup of the cooking liquid. Add the pasta to the frying pan and stir to coat with the sauce. The sauce should be just thick enough to coat the pasta with a little remaining at the bottom of the pan. If the sauce is very watery, stir the pasta for a few minutes over medium-high heat to thicken the sauce. If the sauce is very thick and gloppy, add the reserved 1/4 cup cooking liquid and cook until the sauce is the right consistency. (The spinach and tomato should have added enough liquid to give you a nice thickness, but depending on your heat and pan, you may need to adjust.)

> Dump the whole mess into a large pasta bowl. Sprinkle with the pepper and the cheese, and toss. Serve immediately.

✳ What is al dente, and how do I do it?

Nobody likes a limp noodle. That's why you want your cooked pasta to be *al dente*, which is Italian for "to the tooth." It means cooking pasta until it is just tender, but still has texture. How do you do it? Old-school methods called for draining the pasta as soon as it started to float, or throwing spaghetti against the wall, the idea being that it would stick if it was ready. Not only is this unreliable, it's bad for the wallpaper. Generally, boxed pasta's package directions are trustworthy, but I like to taste the pasta as I go (a good practice generally in anything you're cooking). A couple of minutes before the noodles are supposed to be finished, I'll fish one or two of them out with a pasta fork, blow on it, and chew. If it's at all chalky in the center, it's not done yet.

Sesame–peanut noodles

This is a real favorite in my house. I've adapted it from a recipe in one of my favorite collections, *The New Basics Cookbook,* by Julee Rosso and Sheila Lukins, my copy of which has a broken spine and is so stained it's hard to read (Sesame Chicken and Asparagus Pasta, page 141). In my little variation, you can add cooked chicken or shrimp or asparagus, or you can just do it as is.

I like it with soba noodles, a Japanese-style noodle made from buckwheat, but you can make it with penne, fettuccine, or farfalle, too.

SERVES 4 / WINE PAIRING: Riesling Kabinett or Vouvrag Demi-Sec

Kosher salt for boiling pasta
1/4 cup sesame seeds
1/4 cup peanut butter
1/4 cup toasted sesame oil
1/3 cup roasted peanuts, cashews, or whatever nuts you have
1/3 cup low-sodium soy sauce
1 tablespoon red wine vinegar
1 tablespoon mirin or sherry (see Note)
2 medium garlic cloves
1/4 teaspoon crushed red pepper flakes (or more if you like it spicy)
1 English cucumber (also called hothouse cukes—the long skinny ones), peeled
1 pound soba noodles
1/4 cup chopped fresh cilantro
1/4 teaspoon freshly ground black pepper
3 scallions, green parts only, sliced 1/4 inch thick on an angle

> Bring a large pot of salted water (1 teaspoon salt per quart of water) to a boil.

> Meanwhile, toast the sesame seeds in a dry skillet over medium heat, stirring frequently, until they turn golden brown, about 5 minutes.

> In a food processor, combine the peanut butter, sesame oil, peanuts, soy sauce, vinegar, mirin or sherry, garlic, and red pepper flakes. Process to a purée. Stir in half the toasted sesame seeds.

> Cut the cucumber in half lengthwise and scoop out the seeds with a spoon; discard the seeds. Slice the cucumber halves crosswise about 1/4 inch thick; set aside.

> When the water comes to a boil, add the noodles and cook until tender, 4 to 5 minutes. Drain very well, shaking the colander until it stops dripping, and dump into a bowl. Add the peanut mixture, cilantro, and black pepper, and toss to coat. Turn out onto a large platter. Arrange the cucumber slices around the edge of the platter, sprinkle the scallions on top, and sprinkle the remaining sesame seeds on last. Serve warm or at room temperature.

NOTE: Mirin is a sweetened Japanese rice wine; you'll find it in the Asian section of your supermarket.

Paella with seafood, chicken, and chorizo

This is a magnificent way to feed a crowd. And somehow, it's pretty easy, if time-consuming. Jarred pimientos are available in the International section of your super-market, but you can also use roasted red peppers. You'll need either a paella pan—a very wide, shallow round pan with a lid—or a small roasting pan, or a 9 × 13-inch baking dish and some foil. If you've never cooked with saffron, now's your chance. By weight, it's the most expensive spice in the world (saffron is the three stigmas inside a certain tiny crocus flower from Iran or Spain, and harvesting them is on the tedious side). But it takes only a little bit to turn your rice a brilliant yellow color and to fill the room with an amazing aroma. Serve this with a simple salad, such as the mesclun affair on page 54.

SERVES 6 TO 8 / WINE PAIRING: Rich white Rioja or juicy red Rioja

1 dozen clams

1 dozen mussels

1 tablespoon extra-virgin olive oil

5 bacon slices (about $1/3$ pound), sliced crosswise $1/2$ to $3/4$ inch wide

2 chicken legs

2 chicken thighs, halved crosswise through the bone

2 chicken breast halves on the bone, halved crosswise through the bone

$3/4$ teaspoon kosher salt

$1/4$ teaspoon freshly ground black pepper

2 medium onions, chopped

5 medium garlic cloves, minced

2 cups Valencia rice (a short grain rice from Spain) or Arborio rice

1 jar (17 ounces) roasted sliced pimientos with juice, sliced

1 teaspoon crushed saffron threads

$3^{1}/2$ cups canned low-sodium chicken stock

$1/2$ pound raw chorizo sausage, sliced crosswise $1/2$ inch thick

$1/2$ pound large uncooked shrimp, peeled and deveined (see sidebar, page 60)

1 cup frozen green peas, thawed

Lemon wedges, for serving

> Preheat the oven to 450°F.

> Scrub the clams and mussels under cold running water with a stiff brush to get rid of any sand. If the mussels have "beards" (hairy strings hanging out of the shells), pull those off as best as you can. Throw out any clams that are open. For any open mussels, you can gently close them; if they stay closed they're still fine, otherwise throw them out. Refrigerate the shellfish while you make the rest of the dish.

> In a large paella or frying pan, heat the olive oil over a medium-high flame. Add the bacon and cook until the fat is rendered, about 6 minutes. Transfer the bacon to paper towels and drain, reserving the fat in the pan.

> Arrange the chicken pieces skin side up on a cutting board. Stir together the salt and pepper in a small bowl and sprinkle half of that mixture over the chicken pieces. Bring the pan back up to medium-high, put in the chicken pieces skin side down, and sprinkle with the rest of the seasoning. Cook until brown, turning once, about 5 minutes per side. Remove the chicken from pan and set aside.

> In the same pan, brown the sausage over medium-high heat, about 8 minutes. Remove the sausage to drain on paper towels and discard the fat left in the pan.

> Add the onions and garlic to the pan, turn the heat down to medium, and sauté until the vegetables are beginning to brown, about 10 minutes, scraping up any browned bits. Stir in the rice, roasted pimientos with juice, saffron, and chicken stock, and bring the mixture to a simmer. Simmer 1 minute and remove from the heat.

> Now, if you're using a paella pan, you can go right ahead and arrange the chicken, chorizo slices, shrimp, clams, and mussels on top of the rice mixture. (If you've been working with a frying pan, you'll need to transfer the rice mixture first to a larger pan—something that will hold all of the meats and shellfish in close to a single layer. A small roasting pan will work; a 9 × 13-inch baking dish will work, too. Spoon the rice mixture into that pan or dish, and then add the meats and shellfish.) Sprinkle with the reserved bacon and the peas. Cover with the lid (or foil, if applicable) and bake until the shrimp is cooked through, the clams and mussels have opened, and the rice is tender, about 40 minutes (discard any clams and mussels that fail to open). Uncover the baking dish and let the paella stand for 10 minutes. Serve with lemon wedges.

Pasta en brodo

Pasta served in a pool of rich chicken broth, garnished with pieces of chicken, green beans, fresh herbs, and a healthy handful of grated Parm: This is the simplest of dishes, fresh and light. If we were living in the Italian countryside, as we should be, we'd be making this with a homemade stock. I've poached chicken thighs in canned stock here to kick up the flavor a bit—much quicker than moving to Italy. You'll end up with a few cooked chicken thighs; use them for chicken salad or risotto or something. The pasta shape is entirely optional—pappardelle would be nice, too.

SERVES 4 / WINE PAIRING: Prosecco

Kosher salt for boiling pasta
6 cups canned low-sodium chicken stock
6 skinless chicken thighs, about 2 pounds
2 garlic cloves, halved
10 black peppercorns
1 bay leaf
1 large sprig of fresh thyme (optional)
1 clove (optional)
1/2 pound green beans, ends trimmed
1 pound farfalle (bow-tie pasta)
1/4 cup extra-virgin olive oil
1/4 teaspoon freshly ground black pepper
2 tablespoons chopped flat-leaf parsley
1 cup freshly grated Parmigiano-Reggiano, plus extra for serving

> Bring a large pot of salted water (1 teaspoon salt per quart of water) to a boil.

> Meanwhile, in a large saucepan, combine the chicken stock, chicken thighs, garlic cloves, peppercorns, bay leaf, and thyme and clove, if using. Bring to a boil, reduce the heat to low, and simmer, partially covered, for 30 minutes to cook the chicken. There's going to be some unpleasant-looking gray foam that rises to the top. Skim that off with a ladle or large spoon and discard. (But don't skim the peppercorns and clove.) You'll need to do this a couple of times during the process.

> Remove the chicken with a slotted spoon. Strain the stock through a fine strainer into a clean saucepan, and boil to reduce to 4 cups, about 10 minutes. Bone two of the chicken thighs and shred the meat; set the meat aside. Wrap and refrigerate the remaining chicken for another use.

> When the pasta water comes to a boil, add the beans and cook for 5 minutes, or until tender. Remove with a slotted spoon to a colander and refresh them with cold water to keep the bright green color. Then pat dry, cut into 1-inch pieces, and set aside.

> Add the farfalle to the boiling water and cook until not quite tender, about 8 minutes. (You want to undercook the pasta slightly because it will cook further in the stock.) Drain and discard the pasta water.

> To serve, pour the reduced stock into the pasta pot. Add the green beans, shredded chicken, and olive oil, and bring to a simmer. Add the farfalle, ground pepper, and the parsley, and toss over medium heat for 30 seconds to warm the pasta and cook it completely. Remove from the heat. Use a slotted spoon to divide the pasta, chicken, and beans among 4 large, deep pasta plates. Ladle about one quarter of the stock into each bowl (you might not use all of the stock) and sprinkle each with $1/4$ cup of the cheese. Serve immediately with extra cheese.

Risotto with asparagus, radicchio, and carrots

A great vegetarian option. Radicchio is usually eaten raw in a salad, but its slightly bitter flavor is delicious cooked, too, and it adds an unusual color. Risotto is easy to make once you get the hang of it—and variations are virtually infinite. Try peas and julienned squash in place of the radicchio and carrots below.

SERVES 2 AS AN ENTRÉE, 4 AS AN APPETIZER / WINE PAIRING: Gavi or Verdicchio

7 cups canned vegetable stock

1 cup asparagus pieces (about $1^{1}/_{2}$ inches long), preferably from pencil-thin asparagus, ends trimmed (about $1/3$ bunch)

1 cup carrot half-rounds (carrots halved lengthwise, then sliced thin), from about 3 medium carrots

2 tablespoons extra-virgin olive oil

$1/2$ medium head of radicchio, roughly chopped (into 1-inch pieces)

$1/4$ teaspoon kosher salt, plus more to taste

$1/4$ teaspoon freshly ground black pepper

$1/4$ cup fresh basil leaves, torn into pieces

1 medium onion, chopped

$1^{1}/_{2}$ cups Arborio rice

$2/3$ cup dry white wine, such as a Pinot Grigio

2 tablespoons unsalted butter

$1/2$ cup freshly grated Pecorino cheese, plus extra for serving

2 tablespoons chopped fresh chives or scallions

> Bring the stock to a simmer in a large saucepan. Add the asparagus and carrots and cook until just tender, about 3 minutes. Remove with a slotted spoon to a plate. Turn the heat down under the stock as low as possible to keep it warm.

> Heat 1 tablespoon of the oil in a large saucepan over a medium-high flame. Add the radicchio, sprinkle with $1/8$ teaspoon salt and pepper, and cook, stirring, until lightly browned and wilted, about 2 minutes. Just before the radicchio is cooked, add the basil and stir. Dump the mixture onto the plate with the other vegetables.

RECIPE CONTINUES

> Add the remaining tablespoon of oil to the pan. Add the onion, sprinkle with another 1/8 teaspoon salt, and cook until softened, about 2 minutes. Add the rice and stir to coat with the oil. Add the wine and simmer until almost dry, 1 to 2 minutes.

> Add about 1/2 cup of the warm stock (see Note), stir well, and cook until the rice has absorbed almost all of the stock. Adjust the heat so that the mixture simmers gently, and cook until there's still a little liquid left in the pan but the rice has absorbed most of it; the rice should be neither swimming in liquid nor dry. You don't need to stir constantly: Stir well when you add a new batch of stock, but then you can turn your attention to something else. Just make sure you stir a couple of times before adding more stock. Continue adding stock, about 1/2 cup at a time, stirring and cooking, until most of the stock is absorbed and the rice is al dente—that means it is tender and creamy but with texture. You might not use all of the stock. This should take about 20 minutes, but it might take longer, depending on your heat.

> Stir in the vegetables, butter, cheese, and chives or scallions. Season with 1/8 teaspoon pepper, taste for salt, and serve immediately with extra cheese.

NOTE: A 4- or 6-ounce ladle is very convenient for transferring the stock. You don't want to be measuring piping-hot liquid with a short-handled measuring cup—that's got Burn Unit written all over it.

Risotto with mushrooms, prosciutto, and pecorino

In Italy, risotto is served as a first course, but here in the States it's often a one-pot meal. Make sure people will be seated and ready to eat when the risotto is done; it doesn't wait well. (Mounding it in a bowl helps to retain heat.) In a pinch, though, risotto can be partially cooked ahead of time and held, as is done in restaurants: Cook until the rice is still crunchy and you have added all but 2 or 3 ladles of stock, then stop. Finish cooking at the last minute. Ordinary white button mushrooms are bland, but they could work here as a last resort.

SERVES 2 AS AN ENTRÉE, 4 AS AN APPETIZER / WINE PAIRING: New Zealand Sauvignon Blanc or Italian Arneis

7 cups canned low-sodium chicken stock

3 tablespoons extra-virgin olive oil

2 medium garlic cloves

1 pound assorted mushrooms (portobello, shiitake, cremini)

3/8 teaspoon kosher salt, plus more to taste

3 tablespoons chopped flat-leaf parsley

1/4 teaspoon freshly ground black pepper

1 medium onion, chopped

1 1/2 cups Arborio rice

½ cup dry white wine, such as a Pinot Grigio
2 tablespoons unsalted butter
4 thin slices of prosciutto, torn into pieces
½ cup freshly grated Pecorino cheese, plus extra for serving

> Bring the stock to a simmer in a saucepan; turn the heat down as low as possible.

> Heat 2 tablespoons of the oil in a large saucepan over a medium flame. Add the garlic and cook until softened, 1 to 2 minutes. Add the mushrooms, sprinkle with ¼ teaspoon salt, and cook, stirring every now and then, until the mushrooms are tender and all of the liquid has evaporated, about 8 minutes. Stir in the parsley, season with ⅛ teaspoon pepper, and taste for salt. Dump the mixture into a bowl.

> Heat the remaining tablespoon of oil in the saucepan over medium heat. Add the onion, sprinkle with ⅛ teaspoon salt, and cook until softened, about 2 minutes. Add the rice, stir to coat with the oil, and cook for about 3 minutes, or until translucent. Now add the wine and cook, stirring, until almost dry, 1 to 2 minutes.

> Add about ½ cup of the warm stock (see Note, opposite), stir well, and let cook until the rice has absorbed almost all of the stock. Adjust the heat so that the stock simmers gently with the rice, and cook until there's still a little liquid left in the pan but the rice has absorbed most of it; the rice should be neither swimming in liquid nor dry. You don't need to stir constantly, just frequently: Stir well when you add a new batch of stock, but then you can turn your attention to something else. Just make sure you stir a couple of times before you add more stock. Continue adding stock, about ½ cup at a time, stirring and cooking, until most of the stock is absorbed and the rice is al dente—that means it should be tender and creamy but with texture. You might not use all of the stock. This should take about 20 minutes, but it might take longer, depending on your heat.

> Stir in the reserved mushrooms, butter, prosciutto, cheese, and ⅛ teaspoon pepper. Taste for seasoning and serve immediately with more grated cheese.

4 / The cookout

Ah . . . men and fire. Grilling is the most primal and manly of the culinary arts (not to disparage cake decorating or anything). I never appreciated the majesty of the grill more than the day my friend John Peterson brought home his altar to beef and fire in Chicago. It was 6 feet wide and 2½ feet deep, and you could easily roast a good-size pig on it. Hell, you could have roasted John on it.

Grilling is the easiest and best way to entertain a big crowd because the mess happens outside your kitchen. You'll probably still have some pots and pans to clean up afterward, but most of the action — particularly the greasy, smoky action — happens in the great outdoors. You can even get away without washing the plates and glasses; a cookout is a perfectly acceptable time to use disposable plates and plastic cups. (But get the good ones, the rigid plates that won't get soggy and cause people to drop your cooking on their laps or the lawn, and use real flatware. Those flimsy plastic forks snap, and the knives can't cut anything.) Weight-conscious folks love grilled food, too, because it doesn't require adding fat, and the grill adds so much flavor that you can forgo making rich sauces. (Of course you can also put a compound butter on your steak, as is your right.)

A lot of people are into gas grills these days, and I don't blame them for loving the convenience. I'm a confirmed charcoal man myself, because I believe there's no substitute for the genuine, smoky, char-grilled flavor you can get only from burning a wood product. But gas is easier, particularly for those hardy folk who live in cold climes and who like to grill year round. You can cook these recipes on either gas or charcoal.

Grilled salmon with lemon and herbs

A simple marinade for grilled salmon. It's a little tricky to cook a whole side of salmon because once you put it on the grill you don't want to have to move it around—it has a tendency to fall apart, into the fire. The keys are to make a medium fire; to keep the skin on the fillet (the skin will hold it together even when it's cooked); and to use a squirt gun to put out any fires. Lentils are a classic pairing with salmon, so try the recipe on page 168 as a side dish.

SERVES 6 TO 8 / WINE PAIRING: New Zealand Sauvignon Blanc or Spanish Alborino

2 ½- to 3-pound salmon fillet, with skin
2 tablespoons extra-virgin olive oil
1 tablespoon fresh lemon juice (from about ½ lemon)
2 garlic cloves, chopped
1 teaspoon chopped fresh thyme
1 tablespoon chopped flat-leaf parsley
1 teaspoon kosher salt
½ teaspoon freshly ground black pepper
⅛ teaspoon cayenne pepper
Lemon wedges, for serving

> Working from the fat end to the tail end, run your hand down the center of the salmon fillet to feel for pin bones—the thin, white, flexible bones that run down the length of the fillet. If you find any, the easiest way to remove them is with needle-nosed pliers: Grab the ends of the bones with the pliers and pull. If you don't have pliers, use a paper towel (to get a grip) and your fingers.

> In a small bowl, stir together the oil, lemon juice, garlic, thyme, parsley, salt, pepper, and cayenne. Put the salmon on a baking sheet, skin side down, and spread the mixture all over the flesh. Cover and refrigerate for 1 hour.

> When you're ready to cook, heat a gas grill to medium or dump a pile of briquettes on one half of your charcoal grill so that you have a pile that reaches almost up to the grilling grate. Light the briquettes and let them burn until completely covered with gray ash; this will take from 20 to 30 minutes, depending on whether you're using charcoal briquettes (30 minutes) or hardwood charcoal, which takes only about 20 minutes (see Charcoal, page 84). Spread the coals over about two thirds of the grill, put the grate on top, and let the coals burn down to a medium heat. (Hold your hand about 5 inches above the grill grate. When you can hold it there for only 3 to 4 seconds, you have got a medium fire.) Brush the grate well and use a pair of tongs to clean it again with a wad of paper towels drizzled with oil.

> Put the salmon, skin side up, on the grill and let it cook without messing with it for 5 to 6 minutes, or until you've got an even, golden brown crust and the fish detaches easily from the grill grate. You don't want to have to move this thing until it's ready, so if the fire flares up, use a squirt gun to put out the flame. Using 2 spatulas,

carefully roll the fish over to the skin side. Then use the spatulas to move the fish where you want it to be. (It will move easily; the skin side won't stick.) Cook for another 5 to 6 minutes, until the salmon is almost completely opaque but still translucent in the center. Remove the fish to a platter with the 2 spatulas. Cut into portions with a large, slender knife, or let guests serve themselves with a large spoon. Serve hot or at room temperature with lemon wedges.

+ *VARIATION:* **Grilled Salmon with Charmoula Sauce**
Marinate the salmon in half of one recipe of Moroccan Charmoula Sauce (page 105) for 2 hours. Grill as in the recipe above and serve with the remaining sauce on the side.

Rosemary grilled leg of lamb with honeyed yogurt

I love lamb in almost any form. The high-quality lamb we're getting from Colorado and New Zealand today has a great flavor and certainly doesn't need to be masked with mint jelly or anything else. Butterflying is a butchering technique whereby several cuts are made in the meat so that it can be opened up to lie flat on the grill and cook evenly. Legs of lamb are a good candidate for this technique because once boned, the leg has lots of bumps and lumps (various muscles) that cook differently so people can choose slices cooked to their desired doneness. Butterflying the leg evens out the thickness of the meat, which makes it easy to cook evenly and quickly.

A whole leg of lamb will serve 10 to 12 people; I've used half a leg here because a smaller piece of meat is easier to manipulate, and the sirloin half is more tender than the shank end. Once you get the hang of it, try a whole leg (use the same amount of marinade). In any event, ask your butcher to bone the leg and butterfly it for grilling.

Serve the lamb as is, with Cucumber Yogurt Dip (page 24), or with Green Herb Sauce (page 104).

SERVES 6 TO 8 / WINE PAIRING: Ripe Grenache from Southern France or lush Cabernet Franc

4 to 4½ pounds boned leg of lamb (the sirloin half of a leg), butterflied

3 to 4 large garlic cloves, thinly sliced

3 cups whole-milk or low-fat yogurt

¼ cup honey

¼ cup fresh rosemary needles

1 teaspoon kosher salt

1 teaspoon coarsely ground black pepper

> Make 15 to 20 slits total on both sides of the leg with a thin knife, about 1 inch deep. Shove a slice of garlic into each slit.

> Stir together the yogurt and honey in a baking dish. Crush the rosemary needles in your hand to bruise them (this will release their flavor) and add them to the dish. Stir to combine. Sprinkle the lamb all over with the salt and pepper and put it in the dish; turn it in the marinade to coat completely. Cover and refrigerate for at least 2 hours, or overnight. Turn it once if you remember.

> When you're ready to cook, heat a gas grill to medium or dump a pile of briquettes on one half of your grill, so that you have a pile that reaches almost up to the grilling grate. Light the briquettes and let them burn until completely covered with gray ash; this will take from 20 to 30 minutes, depending on whether you're using charcoal briquettes (30 minutes) or hardwood charcoal, which takes only about 20 minutes (see Charcoal, page 84). Scrape some of the briquettes off the pile so that there is a large pile of charcoal on one side of the grill and a thinner layer of charcoal next to it, graduating to an area with no charcoal at all. Put the grate back on the grill and let it heat up for a few minutes while you attend to the lamb: Scrape most of the yogurt mixture off the leg with a rubber spatula and cut the leg in half so that you have two manageable pieces.

> Brush the grill grate well and use a pair of tongs to clean it again with folded paper towels drizzled with oil.

> Put the lamb, fat side down, on the cooler side of the grill (the side with few briquettes) and cook until well browned, about 5 minutes. Watch the lamb pretty closely, checking it often. If it browns too fast, pull it away from the big pile of coals and deeper into the cooler area of the grill. If it begins to flame, pull it off the heat entirely and then move it back to a cooler area to continue cooking. The honey will burn easily.

> Rotate the lamb about halfway through the cooking, moving the edge facing the hot part of the grill to the other direction, away from the heat. After the lamb has cooked for 5 more minutes, turn the meat and cook, rotating once as above, until an instant-read thermometer stuck into the thickest part of the meat registers 125°F. for rare to medium rare, about 25 minutes. Remove the lamb to a platter and let rest, tented in aluminum foil, for at least 10 minutes (it will stay warm up to about 30 minutes). Then cut into slices on an angle (if you cut straight down you'll get skinny little pieces), across the grain, and serve.

✳ Charcoal

If you're working with charcoal, you first need to decide what kind you want to cook with. Choose between regular briquettes and the lighter-weight, hotter-burning charcoal called "natural hardwood" charcoal.

Briquettes are available at every supermarket. They take slightly longer to start (about 30 minutes) than hardwood, burn less hot, but burn longer. If you use briquettes, I recommend lighting them with what is called a *chimney starter* rather than with traditional lighter fluid, which gives your food a funny taste. A chimney starter is a cylindrical (ergo *chimney*) metal tool with a wooden handle. The chimney itself is divided into two chambers. You fill the upper chamber with briquettes and set the device on the bottom grate of the grill. Then wad up a bunch of newspapers and stuff them into the bottom chamber. Light the newspaper. The starter will hold the flame long enough for the charcoal to light, and eventually the charcoal will flame. Let the flames die down a bit and then dump the charcoal out onto the grate. If the charcoal is completely gray, you probably have a "hot" fire; if the charcoal is still black in places, let it burn until gray.

If you find yourself running out of fire before your food is cooked, you can start a new fire in the chimney on the side of the grill in the same way; but you'll need 20 to 30 minutes lead time. When the new briquettes are ready, remove the grill grate, add them to your dying fire, and go on cooking.

Hardwood charcoal looks like the charred pieces of wood left in a campfire after it has burned out. It catches very quickly (about 20 minutes), burns very hot, but burns out relatively quickly. Hardwood gives a cleaner flavor than briquettes because there are no extra ingredients in the charcoal. To light hardwood, tuck two Weber-brand Fire Starters lighter cubes into your pile of charcoal (one on each side of the mound) and light them. Let the charcoal burn until covered with gray ash.

Although hardwood burns out more quickly than briquettes, that's easy to remedy if you keep your eye on the fire. When you see it starting to die, scatter a new layer of charcoal over the top, in one area, not thick enough to smother the fire underneath. It will catch within 10 minutes—then you just redistribute the new charcoal, and you have a new fire.

★ The world's fastest grilling instructions

Many a great treatise has been written on grilling, and you might want to read one. My goal here is to get you started—now!

CLEAN THE GRATE: Put the grate on the grill and clean it well with a grill brush. Then drizzle some oil on folded paper towels and wipe the grate to clean and oil it completely. Remove the grate and set aside.

LIGHT THE FIRE: If you're working on a gas grill, light it according to the manufacturer's instructions. You need to preheat it just as if you were using an oven. Figure at least 10 minutes, but 15 is better.

If you're working on a charcoal grill, remove the grate. Dump a big pile of charcoal on half of your grill, making a pile that reaches almost up to the grate.

Now light the charcoal, using an electric starter or chimney, and let it burn until covered with gray ash, about 30 minutes for charcoal briquettes, 20 minutes for hardwood charcoal.

ARRANGE THE CHARCOAL: The most important thing is to give yourself a range of heat so that you can move your food from high heat to lower heat as necessary. Equally important, if your food catches fire you can pull it off the heat entirely before it incinerates. It's also handy to have a squirt gun to squelch flare-ups.

When your charcoal is covered with gray ash, use a piece of grilling or fireplace equipment—tongs or a fireplace shovel, for instance—to scrape some of the briquettes off the pile so that there is a large pile of charcoal on one side of the grill, a thinner layer of charcoal next to it, and then an area with no charcoal at all. Now you have a dual-heat fire: hot and not so hot, as well as an area with no direct heat. This allows you to sear meat on the hot part of the grill, and then pull it off to finish cooking on the cooler part. Or, if you find your food cooking too fast, pull it off the heat; if it cooks too slowly, pull it to the hot side.

GAUGE THE HEAT OF THE FIRE: Sometimes you want to cook over a hot fire—when you're searing a steak, for instance. For chicken and fish or a large cut of meat such as a leg of lamb, you're better off cooking over medium heat. To gauge how hot the fire is, hold your hand about 5 inches over the grill grate. If you can hold it there comfortably for only 2 seconds, that's a hot fire; 3 to 4 seconds is medium heat; and 5 to 6 seconds is low heat.

Mustardy barbecued spareribs

I'm partial to the style of barbecue that uses a spice rub and a vinegar sauce rather than the sweet, tomatoey, ketchupy style. I also really love the spicy kick of hot mustard, so I use a little dry Colman's mustard in the rub and some of the prepared mustard in the sauce. This is a great recipe for a crowd because you can prebake the ribs the day before and then just reheat them on the grill.

SERVES 6 TO 8 / WINE PAIRING: California Zinfandel

for the barbecue rub

1 tablespoon kosher salt

1/4 cup sugar

1 tablespoon chili powder

1 tablespoon paprika or other ground chili, such as ancho

3 tablespoons ground cumin

2 teaspoons Colman's dry mustard

1/4 teaspoon ground allspice

for the ribs and sauce

2 3 1/2-pound racks of spareribs

1/2 cup cider vinegar

1/2 cup medium-weight beer, such as Sierra Nevada Pale Ale

1 teaspoon sugar

2 teaspoons Colman's prepared mustard

1 teaspoon kosher salt

> Preheat the oven to 300°F.

> In a small bowl, combine all the rub ingredients. Rub the ribs all over with the dry spice mixture, place them in a roasting pan or on a baking sheet, put them in the oven, and let them roast for 2 hours, or until very tender. They are now completely cooked and can be refrigerated for 2 or 3 days, or until you're ready to serve.

> When you're ready to grill, heat a gas grill to medium or dump your briquettes on one side only of a charcoal grill so that you have a pile that reaches a couple of inches below the grilling grate. Light the briquettes and let them burn until completely covered with gray ash, 20 to 30 minutes, depending on whether you're using char-coal briquettes, about 30 minutes, or hardwood charcoal, about 20 minutes (see Charcoal, page 84).

> Scrape some of the coals off the pile so that the charcoal covers about two thirds of the grill and one third of the grill has no charcoal at all. Put the grill grate on top and let it heat up while you go collect the ribs. Brush the grate well with a grill brush and use a pair of tongs to clean it again with a wad of paper towels drizzled with oil. Let the charcoal burn down to a medium heat. (Test the heat by holding your hand 5 inches above the grill grate; when you can hold your hand there for 3 to 4 seconds,

the fire is medium.) Put the ribs directly over the charcoal and grill slowly, turning once, until the ribs are heated through and have developed a crust, about 20 minutes. If the ribs flame, pull them off the heat or douse the flaming coals with a squirt gun; then put the ribs back over the heat.

> Meanwhile, stir together all the ingredients for the sauce. When the ribs are ready, cut between the bones with a large knife to cut them into individual ribs. Brush with the sauce and serve the remaining sauce on the side.

The ultimate burger is a lambburger

If you love hamburgers, but feel like you need something just a little different, a little more interesting—if you're in a hamburger rut—here's your answer: a *lamb*burger, made with ground lamb from the leg.

For those who are not fans of lamb, you'll also find a beef variation below. The secret to a great beef burger is to use ground chuck, not sirloin, because the fat in chuck gives you a juicier, tastier burger. The other secret is to press the patties together gently, without overly compacting the meat, so it retains a tender texture.

SERVES 8 / WINE PAIRING: Medium-bodied Bordeaux or a heavy-bodied Rosé

3 pounds ground lamb

2 garlic cloves, minced

1 tablespoon tiny (nonpareil) capers

2 tablespoons chopped flat-leaf parsley

2 teaspoons grated lemon zest (from 2 large lemons)

4 teaspoons Dijon mustard

2 teaspoons kosher salt

1/2 teaspoon freshly ground black pepper

8 hamburger buns

Cucumber Yogurt Dip (page 24)

8 large tomato slices

> In a medium bowl, combine the lamb, garlic, capers, parsley, lemon zest, mustard, salt, and pepper. Work the seasonings into the lamb with a spoon or your hands. Form gently into 8 patties; don't pack the meat too tightly.

> Heat a gas grill to medium-high or dump a bunch of briquettes on one side *only* of a charcoal grill, so that you have a pile that reaches a couple of inches below the grilling grate. Light the briquettes and let them burn until completely covered with gray ash; this will take from 20 to 30 minutes, depending on whether you're using charcoal briquettes (30 minutes) or hardwood charcoal, which takes about 20 minutes (see Charcoal, page 84).

> Scrape some of the coals off the pile onto the empty side of the grill so that you have a large pile of charcoal on one side of the grill and a thin layer of charcoal next to it, and then a small area with no charcoal at all. Put the grate back on the grill and let it heat up while you get the hamburgers and buns. Brush the grill grate well with a grill brush. Drizzle a wad of paper towels with oil and use a pair of tongs to clean the grate with it as well.

> Brown the burgers on the hot side of the grill for about 2 minutes on each side; move them off the heat immediately if they begin to flame. Then move the burgers onto the cooler side of the grill and cook for another 2 minutes for medium rare, 3 to 4 minutes for medium.

> Open the buns, put them on the cooler side of the grill, and grill until lightly browned on both sides, about 30 seconds each side.

> To serve, put a burger in each bun, add a few spoonfuls of the yogurt salad, put a slice of tomato on top, and close the bun.

+ *VARIATION:* **Lambburgers with Green Chili, Oregano, and Paprika**
Combine the 3 pounds ground lamb and 2 teaspoons minced garlic in a bowl. Add 2 tablespoons chopped fresh oregano; 4 teaspoons minced, seeded, hot green chili; 2 teaspoons paprika; 2 teaspoons kosher salt; and $1/2$ teaspoon freshly ground black pepper. Grill as in the recipe above. Serve with Cucumber Yogurt Dip into which you have stirred $1/4$ cup halved kalamata olives.

+ *VARIATION:* **Lambburgers with Indian Spices**
Combine the 3 pounds ground lamb and 2 teaspoons minced garlic in a bowl. Add $1/3$ cup chopped scallion; 2 tablespoons whole cumin seeds; 1 tablespoon grated fresh ginger; 2 teaspoons kosher salt; $1/2$ teaspoon cayenne pepper; and $1/2$ tea-spoon freshly ground black pepper. Mix and grill the burgers as in the recipe above. Serve with the Cucumber Yogurt Salad, but replace the dill with $1/2$ cup chopped fresh cilantro.

+ *VARIATION:* **My Favorite Hamburger**
This was about the first thing I ever cooked, as a kid, and I still love it. In a bowl, combine 3 pounds ground chuck; $1/2$ cup chopped onion; 4 teaspoons Worcestershire sauce; 2 teaspoons minced garlic, 2 teaspoons kosher salt; and $1/2$ teaspoon freshly ground black pepper. Shape and grill the burgers as in the recipe above. Serve with a choice of lettuce, tomato, mustard, ketchup, and mayonnaise.

5 / Seafood

We are still a nation of meat-and-potatoes men and fish-and-salad women—at least that's been my experience on a certain makeover show. I can't even tell you how many women have told me that the one thing they'd like to change about their man's eating habits is to get him to put down the hamburger just once and take her to a seafood joint. So guys, there it is: a really easy way to get on her good side. You're welcome.

What I love about seafood is that there is such an incredible, extraordinary variety available. It's not all delicate, wimpy food; far from it. There are a lot of fish out there with steak-like texture and heft that grill beautifully: Swordfish, salmon, striped bass, Chilean sea bass, and tuna are all ultra-grillable, and are suitable for those of you who don't want to give up the thrill of sinking your teeth into a thick chunk of protein.

Beyond love of red meat, there are two other issues that I think deter guys from fish. Some fish have a "fishy" taste they don't like. (I hate that the very adjective *fishy* is negative.) And some fish is so delicate that it can be technically difficult to cook. There's truth to both, but there are also ways to get around both.

To the first I say, it's true that seafood spoils more quickly than other protein. This is aggravated by the fact that fish is not always handled properly. There's a simple answer to this: Get to know your fish guy. Whether you're buying from a supermarket or a more upscale fish store, complain if the fish isn't absolutely fresh, and take it back for a refund. They'll get the picture pretty quickly that you want to be taken seriously. If they are a good fish store, they'll respect your attention to quality. And if they don't, stop shopping there. Find some place that will work with you. Then once you buy seafood, eat it the very same day. It does even the freshest fish no good to sit in your refrigerator overnight.

It's also true that some fish *is* delicate. That's what we have ovens for. I used to be nervous about cooking fish at home, until a fish guy at People's Market in Evanston, Illinois, told me this simple principle: "6 ounces, 10 minutes, 400 degrees." This works for almost any kind of fish fillet—notably salmon—even a whole sheet full of them. Just sprinkle with salt and pepper and maybe some herbs, stick it in a baking dish, and put it in the oven. When it's finished, splash a little vinaigrette on each piece, and you've got yourself an entrée.

Grilled shrimp with a sesame dipping sauce

Everything about this recipe is quick—even the marinating time. Marinate these shrimp for no more than 15 or 20 minutes; any longer and the acid in the citrus marinade will begin to "cook" the shrimp and make them tough.

SERVES 4 / WINE PAIRING: Full-bodied Muscadot

for the marinade and shrimp

$^1/_4$ cup low-sodium soy sauce

4 teaspoons sake or dry sherry

1 tablespoon honey

$1^1/_2$ teaspoons toasted sesame oil

1 medium garlic clove, chopped

20 large shrimp (about $1–1^1/_4$ pounds), peeled and deveined, tails left on

for the sesame dipping sauce

$^1/_2$ teaspoon grated fresh ginger

$^1/_4$ cup low-sodium soy sauce

$^1/_4$ cup fresh lime juice (from about 2 limes)

1 teaspoon dark sesame oil

1 small garlic clove, grated

> Light a charcoal grill or preheat a gas grill (see page 85). Soak eight 12-inch-long wooden skewers in water to cover while the grill heats; this will keep them from burning on the grill.

> About 15 minutes before you plan to cook, make the marinade. Combine the soy sauce, sake or sherry, honey, toasted sesame oil, and chopped garlic in a bowl large enough to hold the shrimp. Add the shrimp, stir, and set aside for no more than 20 minutes.

> For the dipping sauce, stir together all of the ingredients in a larger bowl and then divide among 4 small bowls.

> To skewer the shrimp, shove the pointy end of one skewer through the fat end of one shrimp and thread the shrimp down to the bottom of the skewer. Do that with another shrimp and then with 3 more shrimp so that you have 5 shrimp on the skewer. Now take another skewer, and, holdding it parallel to the first skewer, run it through the skinny tail ends of the shrimp, so that each shrimp is skewered at both ends. (This keeps the shrimp from curling and makes them easier to handle. It also looks good.) Do this with all the rest of the shrimp so that you have 4 double skewers holding 5 shrimp each.

> Grill the shrimp, turning once, until they turn from translucent gray to an opaque, pinky orange color and are lightly browned, $1^1/_2$ to 2 minutes per side. (Check the fat end of one of the shrimp. There should be only a hint of gray in the very center.) Serve each skewer with a bowl of dipping sauce.

Oven-steamed salmon

For this recipe, I've adapted a technique from French chef Michel Bras. The salmon is baked at a very low temperature above a pan of boiling water, so the flesh never toughens but remains silky and moist.

SERVES 4 / WINE PAIRING: Riesling Kabinett or a rich Sancerre

4 salmon fillets (1½ to 2 pounds), skinned
Butter for greasing baking sheet
Grated zest of 1 lemon (optional)
½ teaspoon kosher salt

> Position one oven rack in the top position (the upper third) and a second in the bottom (the lower third). Preheat the oven to 250°F.

> Run your fingers over the salmon to check for pin bones, the slender, white, flexible bones that run down the center of the fillet. If you feel any, pull them out with a pair of needle-nose pliers or just use a paper towel to get enough grip to pull them out with your fingers.

> Bring a frying pan of water to a boil on top of the stove and put it on the lower rack.

> Butter a baking sheet. Put the salmon on the sheet and sprinkle with the lemon zest, if using, and salt. Put the baking sheet on the upper rack and bake for 10 minutes. Turn the fish, and bake for 1 more minute. Remove the salmon to plates and serve with Lemon Vinaigrette (see page 96) or Basil Oil (page 103).

★ How to buy fresh fish

How do you know you're buying good fish? I try to get mine at natural markets or those that specialize in the proverbial fruits of the sea—places that have a really high turnover, which means the freshest product. High-quality natural food stores and organic markets are also a good bet, as are any stores that just plain smell clean. A real fishmonger will have staff members who can answer questions and who will tell you what is particularly fresh and good on any given day. If you're buying a whole fish, the eyes shouldn't be too sunken into their sockets, and should still have some clarity. Fish that's been out of the sea for only a short while should still have a faintly slimy feeling on the scales. And fish should smell like the ocean, not like, well, fish. If it stinks, throw it back.

Roasted cod with almonds, parsley, and green olives

From the creature that gave us the codpiece (sort of): a fish with an unappealing name, but a lovely dense texture. I like roasting for cod because it accentuates its flavor and creates a nice crust that contrasts with the soft fish. Use thick cod fillet, often sold as cod "loin." In this recipe, almonds add sweetness and crunch; parsley and olives, punchiness and color.

SERVES 4 / WINE PAIRING: Semi-dry Riesling

¼ cup whole almonds in the skin (that is, not blanched)

¾ teaspoon kosher salt

⅜ teaspoon freshly ground black pepper

½ teaspoon sweet paprika

1½ to 2 pounds cod fillets, 2 inches thick, if possible; or 2 1½-inch-thick
    cod steaks on the bone

3 tablespoons extra-virgin olive oil

½ cup white wine

½ cup canned low-sodium chicken stock

1 tablespoon fresh lemon juice (from about ½ lemon)

¼ cup chopped flat-leaf parsley

¼ cup green olives, chopped

> Preheat the oven to 400°F.

> Put the almonds on a baking sheet and roast until the skins crack, about 10 minutes. Put them on a cutting board and chop very coarse. Set the almonds aside and raise the oven heat to 425°F.

> In a small bowl, combine ¼ teaspoon of the salt, ⅛ teaspoon of the pepper, and the paprika. Put the cod on a cutting board and sprinkle on one side with this mixture. Heat the oil in a large frying pan over a medium-high flame until the oil smokes. Put the cod in the pan in a single layer, seasoned side down, and cook until browned, about 3 minutes. Now remove the pan from the heat and sprinkle the cod with another ¼ teaspoon salt and ⅛ teaspoon pepper. Turn the cod, put the pan in the oven, and cook until the cod "gapes" —that means you can see the large flakes opening—and is no longer translucent in the center, 7 to 8 minutes (5 to 6 minutes if your cod is only 1½ inches thick). Remove the cod to serving plates or a platter.

> Put the pan back on the stove over medium-high heat. Add the wine and cook until reduced by half, 2 to 3 minutes. Add the stock and chopped almonds and any juices that have accumulated on the plate with the cod, and reduce again by half, about 2 minutes; the sauce will thicken. Now add the lemon juice, parsley, and olives, reduce the heat so that the sauce just simmers, and cook for 30 seconds to integrate the flavors. Season with the remaining ¼ teaspoon salt and ⅛ teaspoon pepper. Pour the sauce over the fish and serve.

+ *VARIATION:* **Simplest Roasted Cod with Paprika, Parsley, and Lemon**
Roast the cod as in the recipe above. Remove the cod to plates. If there's a lot of juice in the pan, return it to medium-high heat, bring the juices in the pan to a simmer, add ¼ cup parsley, and simmer for 1 minute, just to thicken the juices. Or, simply stir in the parsley. (Steaks are likely to release more juices than fillets.) Add any juices that accumulate on the plates with the cod. Serve the cod with the pan juices and a wedge of lemon.

+ *VARIATION:* **Roasted Cod with Red Peppers and Green Herb Sauce**
Follow the recipe above, but after the cod has browned for 1 minute on the stove, add 1 red bell pepper that's been stemmed, seeded, and cut lengthwise into eighths; try to get the pepper onto the bottom of the pan, not on top of the cod. Then turn and roast as in the recipe above. Remove the cod from the pan, put the pan over medium heat, and cook for 2 minutes to reduce the cooking liquid and cook the peppers until tender. Serve the cod and pepper pieces with Green Herb Sauce (page 104) and boiled new potatoes.

Crispy oven-fried crab cakes

These crab cakes are great—just ask Oprah. I made them when I appeared with the *QE* guys on her show, and I was honored (relieved, actually) to earn her coveted seal of approval. Like her, I prefer a crab cake to be mostly crab; these use just enough bread to bind the mixture so it's easy to work with. If you're really serious about this dish, get serious about the main ingredient: Call a great seafood restaurant in your hometown, and ask if they'll sell you fresh, *unpasteurized* jumbo lump crabmeat by the pound. It's much sweeter than anything you can buy in a grocery store. (In Chicago, I picked up the meat at Shaw's Crab House on Hubbard Street.) Concerned about the propriety of a cornflake coating? I was, until I tried it. The idea came from a recipe in *Gourmet* magazine, and it's brilliant. The coating is light and crisp; and because the cakes are baked instead of fried, they're much lighter and less greasy than most crab cakes. Serve with the Lemon Vinaigrette below or with a Chipotle Mayonnaise (see page 104).

SERVES 4 / WINE PAIRING: Dry Riesling or fruity Pinot Noir

for the crab cakes

1 pound jumbo lump crabmeat, picked over for shells and cartilage
1/4 cup mayonnaise
1 large egg, beaten
1 tablespoon Dijon mustard
2 small scallions, coarsely chopped (about 2 tablespoons)
2 heaping tablespoons chopped flat-leaf parsley
1/4 teaspoon Old Bay Seasoning (a spice mix for crab boiling)
    or paprika
1/4 teaspoon kosher salt
1/4 teaspoon freshly ground black pepper
1/4 teaspoon Tabasco sauce
1/4 cup coarsely processed fresh bread crumbs (from about 1 slice white
    bread, preferably a dense, country-style loaf, no need to remove crusts)
3 cups cornflakes

for the lemon vinaigrette

1/4 cup fresh lemon juice (from 2 lemons)
1/2 teaspoon chopped fresh oregano (optional)
1/4 teaspoon kosher salt
1/8 teaspoon freshly ground black pepper
1/2 cup extra-virgin olive oil

> In a large bowl, combine the crabmeat, mayonnaise, egg, mustard, scallions, parsley, Old Bay or paprika, salt, pepper, and Tabasco. Stir gently with a fork to combine. Gently stir in the bread crumbs. Cover and refrigerate for at least 30 minutes, or up to 4 hours; this will stiffen the mixture and make it easier to work with.

> Preheat the oven to 400°F.

> Process the cornflakes to coarse crumbs in the food processor and dump them out onto a plate. Form about ⅓ cup of the chilled crab mixture into a 3-inch cake. Gently dredge the cake in the cornflakes, turning once and patting the cornflakes over the cake to completely cover. Place on an unbuttered baking sheet. Make 7 more crab cakes in the same way and put them on the baking sheet. You can cover and refrigerate the crab cakes for up to 4 hours if you like, or put them in the oven and bake until crisp and warmed through, about 15 minutes.

> While the cakes are baking, make the vinaigrette: In a small bowl, combine the lemon juice; oregano, if using; salt; and pepper. Slowly whisk in the oil.

> When the crab cakes are ready, use a spatula to put 2 crab cakes on each of 4 plates, and spoon the lemon vinaigrette over. Serve immediately.

+ *VARIATION:* **Cocktail Cakes**
These also make very nice cocktail food (you can make the cakes ahead, refrigerate, and bake at the last minute), served with a dab of Chipotle Mayonnaise. Make them about 1 inch in diameter, use 4 cups of cornflakes instead of 3, and bake for 8 to 10 minutes.

✳ Testing for doneness

One legitimate complaint about seafood is that it can be unpleasantly dry. It is—when it's overcooked. The antidote to this problem is to prepare your seafood "lightly cooked." With high-quality seafood, this is perfectly safe—and much more delicious. A fish fillet will continue to cook even after you take it off the heat—particularly a flaky fish like halibut or cod. (I don't find this to be as true for really dense seafood such as swordfish, shrimp, or scallops.) So you want to cook fish one step rarer than you'd like to eat it.

To test for doneness, cut into the fillet (with many fish such as cod, snapper, or salmon, just use the knife to separate the flakes) and look into the center. Raw fish is shiny, translucent, and soft. As it cooks, it turns opaque and stiffens. It is done when you can still see some translucency in the center of the fillet. If you take it off the heat at that point and let it sit a few minutes, you'll see that the translucency will disappear. If you find you like the taste of medium-rare fish, pull it off the heat when a bit more of the center is still translucent.

Braised halibut with white wine and mushrooms

This is one of the easiest, fastest ways to cook any lean, white fish fillets or steaks. Try it with snapper, cod, sole, or flounder (see Note). Cooking in a little wine and water makes a savory liquid; butter and/or oil and a few minutes of simmering produces a sauce-like consistency. Once you get the hang of this, you can flavor your sauce with lots of other ingredients: cream, other herbs and spices, cooked vegetables, bacon or ham, and chilies, to name a few. Stock will add more flavor than water, but it isn't crucial. If you have an open can of stock in the fridge, use it up here.

SERVES 4 / WINE PAIRING: Rich White Rioja or rich Viognier

1 tablespoon extra-virgin olive oil

2 tablespoons unsalted butter

1 small shallot, chopped

1 medium garlic clove, sliced

1 heaping tablespoon fresh rosemary needles

4 ounces shiitakes, stemmed and sliced

4 ounces portobellos, stemmed, caps cut into thirds and sliced

4 ounces cremini or white mushrooms, stemmed and sliced

$1/2$ teaspoon kosher salt, plus more to taste

3 tablespoons dry white wine, such as a Pinot Grigio or Sauvignon Blanc

$1/4$ cup canned low-sodium chicken stock or water

$1^{1}/2$ to 2 pounds halibut steaks, 1 to $1^{1}/4$ inches thick

$3/8$ teaspoon freshly ground black pepper, plus more to taste

1 teaspoon fresh lemon juice (from about $1/2$ small lemon)

1 scallion, chopped, for garnish

> Preheat the oven to 375°F.

> In a large ovenproof frying pan, heat the oil and 1 tablespoon of the butter over a medium flame. Add the shallot, garlic, and rosemary and cook until the shallot is softened, but not colored, 1 to 2 minutes. Add all the mushrooms, sprinkle with $1/4$ teaspoon of the salt, and cook until the mushrooms are tender and any liquid in the pan has evaporated, 5 to 8 minutes. Taste for seasoning. Add the wine and stock or water and swirl the pan to incorporate.

> Now set the fish on top of the mushrooms. Sprinkle with another $1/4$ teaspoon salt and $1/4$ teaspoon of the pepper, and dot with the remaining tablespoon of butter. Bring to a simmer over medium heat, cover, put the pan in the oven, and bake until the fish is cooked through, 10 to 12 minutes. Use a knife to look at the flesh near the bone; it should still be translucent in the center.

> Remove the fish to a plate. Set the pan over medium-high heat and simmer until the juices are reduced and thickened to a thin sauce, 2 to 3 minutes. By this time, the fish will have released some liquid; add that to the pan as well and reduce a little more, depending on how much liquid you added. Stir in the lemon juice and the remaining $1/8$ teaspoon pepper and taste for seasoning.

> Put the fish onto serving plates and spoon the mushrooms and sauce over. Sprinkle with the scallions and serve hot.

NOTE: If you're using fillets, fold the tail under the thicker body of the fillet so that the tail doesn't overcook. If you're cooking very thin flounder fillets, fold them in half so that they are double thickness. The thinner the fillet, the shorter the cooking time. Figure as little as 6 minutes for flounder fillets; 7 to 8 minutes for a 1-inch-thick halibut, cod, or hake fillet; and 8 to 10 minutes if the fillet is $1^{1}/_{2}$ inches thick.

+ *VARIATION:* **Braised Fish with Tomatoes and Spices**
Cut 4 large plum tomatoes (about $1^{1}/_{4}$ pounds) in half and squeeze out the seeds over the sink; coarsely chop each half. Heat 2 tablespoons olive oil in the frying pan and cook 1 chopped shallot, 2 sliced garlic cloves, and 4 ounces cremini or white mushrooms as in the recipe above. Remove the pan from the heat. Sprinkle the tomato and 2 bay leaves over the bottom of the pan and season with $1/_2$ teaspoon ground cumin, $1/_2$ teaspoon dried oregano, $1/_4$ teaspoon turmeric, $1/_2$ teaspoon salt, and $1/_8$ teaspoon pepper. Add 2 tablespoons water and swirl to incorporate. Set the fish on top and sprinkle with $1/_4$ teaspoon salt and $1/_8$ teaspoon pepper; drizzle with 1 tablespoon olive oil. Cook, covered, as in the recipe above. When the fish is cooked, remove it from the pan. Add $1/_4$ cup raisins to the pan and reduce the sauce until the liquid around the tomatoes is thickened by about half, 3 to 5 minutes. You might want to splash a little Tabasco in this one.

Sautéed sea scallops with a sesame crust

Scallops, so naturally sweet, go beautifully with sesame oil—one of my favorite ingredients. Sesame seeds make an impressive presentation and add a little crunch. The sautéed spinach on page 160 is an excellent side.

Note that the sauce for this recipe and in all of the variations is intended to be thin. Add 2 tablespoons butter for a thicker, richer sauce.

SERVES 4 / WINE PAIRING: Sancerre or White Bordeaux

$1^{1}/_{2}$ to 2 pounds large sea scallops (see "The Trouble with Buying Scallops," opposite)

$^{1}/_{4}$ to $^{1}/_{3}$ cup sesame seeds, with hull, if possible (see Note)

2 tablespoons extra-virgin olive oil

2 tablespoons unsalted butter

Juice of $^{1}/_{2}$ lemon

$^{1}/_{2}$ cup canned low-sodium chicken stock

2 teaspoons toasted sesame oil

$^{1}/_{8}$ teaspoon freshly ground black pepper

$^{1}/_{4}$ teaspoon kosher salt

1 scallion, chopped, for garnish

> Try to buy scallops that are all about the same size so they cook similarly. When you're ready to cook, check all of the scallops for a small, crescent-shaped opaque white muscle that may be on the side of each. These attach the animal to the shell, and they're tough. Just pull them off and throw them away.

> Put the sesame seeds on a plate. Dip the top of each scallop in the seeds, pat to press the seeds into the flesh, and put the scallops, seed side up, on a plate. In a large frying pan, heat the oil and 1 tablespoon of the butter over a medium flame. When the fat is hot, add the scallops, seed sides down, and cook until the seeds have browned and the scallops detach easily from the pan, 2 to 3 minutes. Then use a thin metal spatula to carefully turn each scallop, and cook on the other side for another 2 to 3 minutes, depending on the size of the scallops. You want the meat to cook enough to firm it, but it should still be creamy. Touch the scallops on the tops and sides while they're cooking to feel how they firm up so that you can train your fingers. And when you suspect that they're about done, cut one open to see—it should still be a little translucent in the center (medium-rare). Don't hesitate to take a bite and see how you like them cooked.

> Remove the scallops to a plate. Some of the sesame seeds will stick to the pan and each scallop won't have a perfect crust. It's okay. Now add the lemon juice and stock to the pan and cook over medium-high heat until reduced by half, 2 to 3 minutes. Stir in the remaining 1 tablespoon of butter, the sesame oil, pepper, and salt. Arrange the scallops on 4 dinner plates and drizzle a couple of spoonfuls of the pan sauce around each pile. Garnish with the chopped scallion and serve.

NOTE: Sesame seeds with the hull (usually *not* the ones sold by large spice companies at the grocery stores, who sell hulled seeds for some reason), seem to stick better to the scallop and less to the pan. They're available at health food stores.

+ *VARIATION:* **Sautéed Scallops with Curry**
Spread 1 tablespoon curry powder over the bottom of a plate and season with $1/4$ teaspoon salt. Dip the tops of the scallops in the curry powder and cook as in the recipe above. Take the scallops out of the pan. Add $1/2$ cup white wine and $1/2$ cup chicken stock and reduce by about half. Stir in 1 tablespoon butter, and 1 tablespoon chopped fresh parsley, cilantro, chives, basil, or a combination. Serve the scallops drizzled with the sauce.

✳ The trouble with buying scallops

A large percentage of scallops are soaked in a chemical solution after harvesting and shucking in order to preserve them. This preservative makes scallops taste funny, which is problematic enough. But the scallops also absorb the liquid, so when you sauté them, the liquid is released into your pan and the scallops won't brown.

In the seafood industry, scallops that aren't soaked are called "dry" scallops, and you may see them sold as such. You can also identify soaked scallops because they are usually very white (dry scallops range in color from off white to beige) and they're bound to be sitting in some of the liquid as it seeps out of the scallop. *Don't* buy soaked scallops. If that's all that is available, change your menu.

Pan-roasted salmon with sweet tomato vinaigrette

You can buy farmed salmon all year round and it is one of your better bets for freshness. But wild salmon from Alaska, Washington, and California is definitely more flavorful, and it's available throughout the summer almost anyplace with FedEx— which is to say, anyplace. Cook 'em if ya got 'em.

SERVES 4 / WINE PAIRING: Fruity Barbera or Verdicchio

for the tomato vinaigrette

1 medium shallot, sliced

2 tablespoons red wine vinegar

1 tablespoon nonpareil capers (the tiny ones), drained

1 pint cherry or grape tomatoes, cut in half lengthwise

1/2 teaspoon kosher salt

1/3 cup extra-virgin olive oil

1/3 cup canola oil

1 tablespoon chopped flat-leaf parsley

1 tablespoon chopped fresh basil

1/2 teaspoon ground cumin

1/8 teaspoon freshly ground black pepper

for the salmon

3 tablespoons extra-virgin olive oil

1 1/2 to 2 pounds salmon fillets, with skin (about 1 1/2 inches thick at the thickest point)

1/2 teaspoon kosher salt

1/8 teaspoon freshly ground black pepper

> Preheat the oven to 425°F.

> Make the vinaigrette: In a medium bowl, stir together the shallot, vinegar, capers, tomatoes, and 1/2 teaspoon salt. Let that stand while you cook the salmon, then stir in the 1/3 cup olive oil, 1/3 cup canola oil, parsley, basil, cumin, and 1/8 teaspoon pepper.

> Heat the 3 tablespoons olive oil in a large, oven-safe frying pan over a medium-high flame. Sprinkle the salmon with the 1/2 teaspoon salt and 1/8 teaspoon pepper. When the oil is hot, add the fillets, skin side up, and cook, without messing with them at all, until they move easily when you shake the pan, about 3 minutes. If you pull them off before they're ready, the browned layer will stick to the pan and you'll lose the beautiful crust. Now turn the salmon and stick the pan in the oven. Roast until just cooked through, 6 to 8 minutes.

> When the salmon is cooked, remove it to serving plates with a spatula. Add the vinaigrette to the pan, put it over medium heat, and bring just to a simmer, stirring with a wooden spoon to pick up the browned bits off the bottom of the pan. Cook until the tomatoes soften, about 2 minutes. Spoon the sauce over the salmon and serve.

Sauces for grilled, baked, and sautéed seafood

You can use these sauces on practically anything with fins, scales, or shells: baked fish, sautéed fish, and grilled fish, certainly. They'll work on other meats as well. For example, the Green Herb Sauce is delicious with the Roasted Pork Shoulder Pernil on page 149. You don't actually need a formal sauce to eat fish: Most seafood tastes delicious finished with a drizzle of good-quality extra-virgin olive oil and a wedge of lemon or lime. A drizzle of soy sauce and sesame oil, or soy and lemon, is another simple way to go; there's something about the taste of the fish that seems to welcome the acidity of citrus and the sharp saltiness of soy sauce. Capers and anchovies, too.

But sometimes we want to show off. So here are a few easy sauces you can make on the side to add to what you'll find in the seafood recipes.

basil oil

MAKES 1¼ CUPS

2 cups fresh basil leaves (from 1 large bunch)
1 medium garlic clove, crushed
1 scallion, coarsely chopped
½ teaspoon kosher salt
⅛ teaspoon freshly ground black pepper
1 cup extra-virgin olive oil

> Bring a medium saucepan of water to a boil. Add the basil leaves and let them sit in the water until they turn bright green, about 15 seconds. Drain in a colander in the sink and immediately run cold water over the basil until chilled. Squeeze out the basil and pat dry between 2 paper towels.

> Put the basil into a blender along with the garlic, scallion, salt, pepper, and about half of the oil. Blend until smooth. Add the remaining oil and blend until combined. Pour into a container and use immediately, or refrigerate for 1 to 2 weeks. Serve with fish.

SAUCES CONTINUE

chipotle mayonnaise

Chipotle chilies are smoked jalapeño peppers that have been packed in a Mexican barbecue sauce called adobo and canned.

MAKES 1 CUP

1 cup mayonnaise
$1^1/_2$ canned chipotle chilies in adobo sauce
1 tablespoon fresh lime juice (from 1 lime)

> Put all of the ingredients into the food processor and purée until smooth. Serve with crab cakes or grilled fish.

green herb sauce

MAKES ABOUT $1^1/_2$ CUPS

$^1/_3$ cup chopped flat-leaf parsley
$^1/_4$ cup chopped fresh cilantro
2 tablespoons chopped fresh basil
2 tablespoons chopped fresh mint
2 tablespoons chopped scallion
1 tablespoon chopped capers
1 medium garlic clove, chopped
1 tablespoon red wine vinegar
$^2/_3$ cup extra-virgin olive oil
$^1/_4$ teaspoon kosher salt
$^1/_4$ teaspoon freshly ground black pepper

> Stir together all the ingredients in a bowl. Serve with fish or meat.

moroccan charmoula sauce

This is Morocco's answer to the green herb sauce; fragrant, pungent, and a little spicy. Works as both a sauce and a marinade for grilled fish.

MAKES ABOUT 1½ CUPS

1 bunch of flat-leaf parsley
1 bunch of fresh cilantro
4 medium garlic cloves, sliced
¾ cup extra-virgin olive oil
6 tablespoons fresh lemon juice (from 3 lemons)
2 teaspoons whole cumin seeds
2 teaspoons whole coriander seeds
1½ teaspoons paprika
½ teaspoon crushed red pepper flakes
½ teaspoon kosher salt
¼ teaspoon freshly ground black pepper

> Working with ½ bunch of parsley at a time, hold the parsley stems, still in a bunch, in your left hand so that the leaves lie on the cutting board. Then holding the blade of a large knife almost parallel to the cutting board and cutting away from you, shave the leaves off the stems with quick, short strokes. You're not cutting down on the stems, but rather making knife strokes that follow the stems with just enough of an angle to catch the leaves and cut them off. You'll need to turn the bunch as you shave each part, and you may need to trim off a little stem still connected to some of the leaves. Continue doing this until you have 1 firmly packed cup of parsley leaves. Discard the stems and dump the leaves into the bowl of a food processor.

> Lay the cilantro on the cutting board and, working with the whole bunch, coarsely chop until you have 1 firmly packed cup. (The top ends of the cilantro stems are tender, so you don't really need to cut the leaves off the stems.) You'll use the better part of a large bunch or all of a small bunch. Put the cilantro in the food processor as well.

> Add the rest of the ingredients and process until the herbs and garlic are chopped, 15 to 30 seconds. Use immediately or refrigerate.

6 / **Poultry**

I love roast chicken, you love roast chicken, and it's one of the easiest ways to put a casually elegant dinner on the table. Back in the all-important Introduction, I gave you a basic recipe for the simplest way I've figured out to roast a whole bird without having to mess with it too much.

I like stuffing chickens with things like herbs, garlic, and lemon to add as much flavor as possible to the meat. I also use an ingredient with a little sugar to help the bird brown; honey works well because it's sweet and thick, and orange juice or maple syrup will do the trick, too. The bits that stick to the bottom of the roasting pan while the chicken cooks make a terrific base for sauces, so I've given you some recipes for quick-and-easy ones.

Beyond the roast chicken are all the delicious dishes made by cooking chicken parts in a liquid, variously called stews, sautés, or braises (see How to Make a Chicken Stew, page 113). They can be made with a whole, cut-up chicken (white and dark meat), with selected chicken parts, or with cutlets. The advantage to cutlets is that they cook very quickly, which makes them excellent fodder for mid-week cooks. To my mind, though, cutlets don't have much taste if they're just sautéed, unless they're first coated with seasoned bread crumbs (see page 124) and pan-fried or otherwise flavored. They do, however, become terrific vehicles for exotic sauces if you cut them up and use them in preparations such as stir-fries, tandoori marinades, kebabs, or a Thai green curry.

✳ How to buy chicken

You might reasonably ask just what, exactly, is an Amish chicken. Or, for that matter, a kosher chicken. An organic chicken? Or a free-range chicken?

I like to joke that I'll only eat chickens that are organically farmed by differently abled Unitarian lesbians of color — it's a joke, I said — but

our concern here is not just the politics of poultry. All four approaches to farming produce a healthier, happier bird with better flavor and texture. Organic farmers use only natural feeds that were themselves farmed organically, and forbid the use of growth-promoting antibiotics. Free-range or cage-free chicken is poultry that's been permitted to walk around; this is more of an issue about animal treatment than one of flavor (factory farming practices are considered cruel by some because birds are often kept in tiny cages). Kosher

chicken is processed under the strict supervision of a rabbinical council that enforces cleanliness, and also requires that the bird be brined in a salt solution (which, happily, gives the meat a terrific flavor, but is something you need to consider before you add more salt). Amish chickens come from Pennsylvania and Ohio, and prefer plain

cotton clothing and wide-brimmed hats — um, that is, they are usually raised free-range, are not usually fed antibiotics, and are medicated only when they're sick.

In any case, any of these types of bird are practically guaranteed to be of higher quality than one that says merely "chicken."

Roasted chicken parts with herbs and lemon

This is essentially my favorite roast chicken recipe, deconstructed into parts, and using thyme instead of tarragon. It's much better if you give it some time to marinate—even just a little bit. Simply dump these few ingredients over the chicken in a pie dish or whatever and let it sit in the refrigerator.

SERVES 4 / WINE PAIRING: French Pinot Noir or New Zealand Sauvignon Blanc

1 lemon

1 tablespoon Dijon mustard

$1/4$ cup plus 1 tablespoon extra-virgin olive oil

3 tablespoons chopped fresh thyme leaves

1 bay leaf, broken in half

$1/4$ teaspoon cracked black peppercorns

$3/4$ teaspoon kosher salt

4 chicken breasts on the bone ($2 1/2$ to 3 pounds), or 4 legs, or some combination
    of favorite parts

> Strip the zest off the lemon with a fine grater or vegetable peeler. Squeeze the juice of half of the lemon into a wide, shallow bowl. (Reserve the other half for later.) Add the mustard and whisk together. Then whisk in $1/4$ cup of the oil, just like you're making a salad dressing. Stir in 2 tablespoons of the thyme, the bay leaf, cracked peppercorns, and $1/2$ teaspoon of the salt. Put the chicken parts in the bowl, add the lemon zest strips, and toss to coat the chicken. Marinate for at least 1 hour and as long as 4.

> Preheat the oven to 425°F.

> Heat the remaining 1 tablespoon olive oil in a large ovenproof sauté pan over a medium flame. Sprinkle the chicken with the remaining $1/4$ teaspoon salt and add it, skin side down, to the pan. Cook until the skin is nicely browned, about 5 minutes. Then turn the pieces, put the pan in the oven, and roast until well browned and cooked through, 25 to 30 minutes.

> Remove the chicken to a platter. Put the pan over high heat and bring to a boil to reduce the juices slightly, 2 to 3 minutes. Stir in the juice of the reserved half of the lemon and the remaining 1 tablespoon thyme. Serve the chicken with the juices.

+ *VARIATION:* **Chicken with White Wine, Lemon, and Herbs**
Mix it up by introducing the punchiness of wine to the sauce. After the chicken is cooked, add $1/2$ cup of whatever white wine you're drinking to the pan, and reduce by half, about 1 minute. Add the lemon, chopped thyme, and 1 teaspoon capers. Stir in a tablespoon or two of butter if you want a richer sauce.

Soy-and-honey glazed roast chicken

The same glaze I use on grilled pork tenderloin is fantastic on roast chicken, too. You need a brush (buy one at the supermarket — or the hardware store, for that matter) so that you can brush the glaze all over the bird; the better you glaze it, the better it looks and tastes. Do it several times while cooking. Serve this with Roasted String Beans with Shallots (page 158).

SERVES 4 / WINE PAIRING: Full-bodied Gavi

for the chicken

1 4- to 4 $1/2$-pound chicken, rinsed inside and out and patted dry with paper towels

1 teaspoon kosher salt

$1/4$ teaspoon freshly ground black pepper

$1/2$ lemon

1 medium head of garlic (or $1/2$ large head)

2 bay leaves

$1 1/2$-inch piece of fresh ginger, peeled, cut into coins, and smashed with the side of a large knife

2 tablespoons unsalted butter, melted

for the glaze

2 tablespoons low-sodium soy sauce

2 teaspoons sake or dry sherry

$1 1/2$ teaspoons honey

$3/4$ teaspoon toasted sesame oil

> Preheat the oven to 400°F. Line a roasting pan with aluminum foil. (Really *do* this — trust me, you don't want to have to clean burnt honey from the pan.) Put a V-rack in the pan, oil the rack with a brush or a paper towel drizzled with oil so that the chicken skin doesn't stick, and put it all in the oven to heat up.

> Cut off any lumps of fat you see around the neck of the chicken. Then balance the bird on the neck end and sprinkle the inside of the cavity generously with the salt and pepper. Put the lemon half into the cavity along with the garlic, bay leaves, and the coins of ginger.

> For the glaze, stir together all of the ingredients in a small bowl.

> When you're ready with the chicken, pull the roasting pan out of the oven. Put your chicken, breast side down, in the hot pan and brush with about half of the butter. Roast for 20 minutes for a 4-pound bird, 25 minues for a 4½ pounder. Then remove the pan from the oven and brush the bird with the glaze. Return the pan to the oven and roast for 20 more minutes, brushing once or twice with the glaze if you feel like it.

> Now take the pan out of the oven again, turn the chicken, and repeat the process: Brush the breast with the remaining butter, stick the bird back in the oven, and roast for 20 minutes for a 4-pound bird, 25 minutes for a 4½ pounder. Then remove from the oven, brush the breast with the glaze, and continue roasting for about 20 more minutes, until an instant-read thermometer inserted into the thickest part of the thigh reads 165° to 170°F. (about 1 hour 20 minutes total for a 4-pound bird, 1½ hours for a larger chicken). Or, stick the tip of a small knife into the thickest part of the thigh: the juices should run clear, not red. Brush the chicken a few times while it's roasting so that the skin gets a really beautiful brown color. (You'll probably find that the chicken browns more evenly if you turn the pan a couple of times during roasting; it depends on your oven.)

> When the chicken is cooked, put it on a plate and let it rest for about 10 minutes. To serve, cut the bird into quarters: Cut between the leg and breast on each side, then down through the hip joints to cut off the legs. Cut along each side of the breast-bone, then push the breast halves off the carcass.

Arroz con pollo

This is simply a very good Mexican chicken stew in which rice is cooked along with the chicken. Cooking cilantro into the rice is not traditional, but the herb, which is controversial among some eaters, has a milder taste when it's cooked, and it flavors the rice beautifully. You'll need either a Dutch oven or a wide, shallow pot with a lid.

SERVES 4 / WINE PAIRING: Spanish Rioja

2 medium onions
1 red bell pepper
4 medium garlic cloves, minced
1 tablespoon chopped fresh oregano
1 bunch of fresh cilantro
$1/4$ cup almonds, with skin
2 tablespoons extra-virgin olive oil
$3/4$ teaspoon kosher salt, plus more to taste
$1/2$ teaspoon freshly ground black pepper
1 chicken ($3^1/2$ to 4 pounds) cut into 10 pieces (see Note)
1 teaspoon whole cumin seeds
1 bay leaf
2 cups long-grain rice
2 teaspoons sweet paprika
3 cups canned low-sodium chicken stock
1 cup frozen petite peas, thawed
$1/4$ cup green pimiento-stuffed olives, cut into halves or thirds
Lime wedges, for serving

> Preheat the oven to 400°F.

> Cut the onions in half through the stem ends. Then cut each half in half again through the equator and slice so that you get thin, short slices. Stem and seed the bell pepper and cut in half crosswise; cut each half lengthwise into 8 pieces. Put the vegetables into a bowl along with the garlic and oregano.

> Rinse the entire bunch of cilantro, put it on a cutting board, and thinly slice across the bunch until you have $3/4$ cup chopped cilantro; you'll have some stem in there, too, but that's fine. Then chop 2 tablespoons extra for garnish. Put the almonds on a baking sheet and roast in the oven for 10 minutes, or until the skins begin to crack. Coarsely chop them and set aside.

> Heat the oil in a Dutch oven or wide, shallow (4 to 5 inches high) pot over a medium flame. In a small bowl, stir together $1/2$ teaspoon salt and $1/4$ teaspoon pepper. Lay the chicken pieces out in a single layer on your board, skin side up, and sprinkle with half of the seasoning; flip the pieces and sprinkle with the rest of the seasoning. Put the chicken in the pan, skin side down, and cook for 5 minutes to brown. Then turn and cook for 5 more minutes to brown the other side. Remove the chicken to a plate with tongs or a slotted spoon.

> Add the cumin to the pan over medium heat and let sizzle in the fat until you can smell it, 30 to 60 seconds. Add the onions, bell pepper, garlic, and oregano, along with the bay leaf and $1/4$ teaspoon salt. Cook, stirring, until the onions are wilted, 5 to 6 minutes. Scrape the bottom of the pan as you cook to release the browned bits; the liquid from the onions should be enough to dissolve the caramelized juices.

> Add the rice and paprika and stir for 1 minute. Add the stock and the $3/4$ cup cilantro and stir to combine. Return the chicken pieces in a single layer, along with any juices that have accumulated on the plate. Bring the stock, uncovered, to a simmer. Now cover the pan, reduce the heat to low, and cook until the liquid has evaporated, about 20 minutes. Gently stir in the peas, olives, chopped almonds, and the remaining $1/4$ teaspoon pepper. Cover and let stand for 5 minutes. Taste for salt (whether you need any at all will depend on how salty the stock is). Sprinkle with the remaining 2 tablespoons cilantro and serve hot, with lime wedges.

NOTE: Have your butcher cut the chicken into 10 pieces: Cut off the wings; cut off the legs and separate them into thighs and drumsticks at the joint. Cut each breast in half crosswise as well.

✕ How to make a chicken stew

More than a recipe, this is a cooking technique for a stew with an intensely flavorful sauce. You can vary it endlessly.

The basic structure is as follows: Brown the chicken in butter or oil, then take it out of the pan. This first step encourages juices from the chicken to caramelize on the bottom of the pan, thus giving you the foundation of a sauce. The next step is to add a liquid over heat such as wine, stock, cream, or even water. The liquid will dissolve the brown bits. Sometimes a vegetable is cooked first—typically onion, shallot, or garlic—and then liquid is added. The water in the vegetable will also dissolve the browned bits. Tomatoes may replace the liquid, as is the case here.

Finally, put the chicken back in the pan along with any herbs or vegetables you choose, cut small enough to cook in 20 minutes. Simmer until the chicken is cooked through. If you want the liquid to reduce, leave the pan uncovered. If you've used a small amount of liquid and want to retain it, cover the pan. When the chicken is cooked, remove it from the pan and simmer the sauce until it has the taste and consistency you like—the more you reduce it, the thicker it gets. Season and garnish with flavorful ingredients such as fresh herbs, olives, lemon zest, or cooked mushrooms, and serve with bread.

Chicken sauté with mushrooms, garlic, and bay leaf

This is a great dish—rustic French comfort food at its best—and it'll impress anyone you're serving. If you can get fresh varietal mushrooms, great (most super-markets sell at least creminis, shiitakes, and portobellos), otherwise the white button ones will work fine, too. But you *have* to use the dried porcinis to get the intense flavor.

SERVES 4 / WINE PAIRING: Early Rhône

$^1/_3$ cup dried porcini mushrooms

$^3/_4$ pound assorted mushrooms (such as white button, shiitake, cremini, and oyster), stemmed and sliced (see Note)

2 tablespoons extra-virgin olive oil

1 tablespoon unsalted butter

$^3/_4$ teaspoon kosher salt, plus more to taste

$^1/_4$ teaspoon freshly ground black pepper, plus more to taste

4 chicken breasts on the bone ($2^1/_2$ to 3 pounds total), cut in half to make 8 pieces

6 medium garlic cloves, in their skins

1 bay leaf

Pinch of crushed red pepper flakes

$^1/_2$ cup dry white wine

1 cup heavy cream

Juice of $^1/_2$ lemon (1 to 2 tablespoons)

$^1/_4$ cup chopped flat-leaf parsley

> Soak the dried porcini mushrooms in enough hot water to cover for about 30 minutes, or until they're soft. Meanwhile, cut up the fresh mushrooms into bite-size pieces and put them in a bowl. When the porcinis are soft, remove them from the water (just use your hand) and squeeze out the excess liquid over the bowl; reserve the soaking liquid for the sauce. Chop the porcinis and put them in the bowl with the fresh mushrooms.

> In a sauté pan large enough to hold the chicken in one layer, combine 1 tablespoon of the oil and the butter over medium heat. In a small bowl, combine $^1/_2$ teaspoon salt and the pepper. Put the chicken on a cutting board and sprinkle all over with the seasoning mixture. When the butter has melted, put the garlic cloves and the chicken in the pan, skin side down, and cook until the skin is good and brown, 12 to 15 minutes. The skin should brown slowly so that lots of those good brown bits accumulate on the bottom of the pan. (This is the stuff that's going to make your sauce taste great; you'll see.) Regulate the heat so that the chicken browns gratifyingly, but not too fast. You should hear a consistent "snap, crackle, and pop" as the chicken cooks, but it shouldn't sound too loud; if the heat is too high, all that

RECIPE CONTINUES

stuff on the bottom of the pan will burn. Move the chicken around so that it browns nicely on the difficult-to-reach areas — you might, for example, want to set one breast on a slight angle, resting on another breast for a minute or two, to brown an edge.

> Once the skin is browned, turn the chicken over and brown for 5 to 10 minutes on the other side — same routine. (The chicken should be pretty well cooked through now. Peek under the tenderloin on the underside of the breast and see if the meat looks raw. If so, keep cooking.) Remove the fully cooked chicken from the pan. Add the remaining tablespoon of olive oil, the reserved mushrooms, the bay leaf, and the red pepper flakes to the pan and cook until the mushrooms give up their liquid, and then the liquid all evaporates; this will only take a few minutes. While the mushrooms are cooking, scrape the bottom of the pan with a wooden spoon to pick up the brown bits. Then turn the heat to medium high and cook until the mushrooms begin to brown, another 2 minutes.

> Move the pan off the heat and sprinkle the mushrooms with the remaining $1/4$ teaspoon salt. Add the wine, and return the pan to the heat. Turn the heat to high and boil until the wine has reduced to a glaze on the bottom of the pan, 1 to 2 minutes. Now pour in the reserved mushroom soaking liquid and cook that down until it is thick and reduced by about two thirds, 1 to 2 minutes. Finally, add the cream and simmer until the sauce has thickened enough to coat the back of a spoon, about 3 minutes. Turn the heat down to low.

> Using tongs, put the chicken back in the pan along with any juices that have collected on the plate, and simmer for a few more minutes to reheat the chicken and blend the flavors in the sauce.

> To serve, put the chicken on 4 serving plates. Stir the lemon juice and parsley into the sauce and taste for salt and pepper. If the sauce appears too thin (it should still coat the back of a spoon), reduce it for a few more minutes, then spoon it over the chicken and serve.

NOTE: The stems of shiitake mushrooms are tough, so they should be removed entirely; pull them off the caps. For all the other mushrooms, just trim the bottoms of the stems. Or, if the mushrooms are a little old and the stems look dark and soft, pull them off completely and throw them away.

Rosemary chicken with summer tomatoes and olives

Cook this when you've got a bowlful of those great end-of-summer tomatoes. Usually tomatoes are peeled before cooking, but sometimes I can't be bothered. Call it texture.

SERVES 4 / WINE PAIRING: New Zealand Sauvignon Blanc

2 pounds ripe tomatoes

2 tablespoons extra-virgin olive oil

2 tablespoons fresh rosemary needles

4 large or 6 medium garlic cloves, smashed with the flat side of a large knife

1 4-pound chicken, cut into 10 pieces

1 teaspoon kosher salt

$1/4$ teaspoon freshly ground black pepper

2 tablespoons red wine vinegar

$1/4$ cup torn fresh basil leaves

$1/2$ cup pitted kalamata olives

> Cut off the stem ends of the tomatoes, then cut the cored tomatoes in half through the equator. Place a fine wire strainer over a medium bowl and squeeze the tomato halves over the strainer to remove the seeds and juice. Then cut the halves into large chunks and set them aside. Press the seeds and juice through the strainer with a spoon or rubber scraper. Discard the seeds and set the juice aside.

> In a 12-inch, deep frying pan or a Dutch oven, combine the oil, rosemary, and garlic. Cook over medium-low heat for 2 minutes to flavor the oil without allowing the garlic to brown.

> Meanwhile, lay the chicken pieces in a single layer on a piece of wax or parchment paper or aluminum foil. In a small bowl, stir together $1/2$ teaspoon of the salt and the pepper. Sprinkle half of the seasoning mixture over the chicken, turn the chicken pieces, and sprinkle with the remaining seasoning mixture. Put the chicken into the pan, skin side down. Turn the heat to medium high and sauté to brown the chicken, 5 to 7 minutes. Then turn the chicken and brown the other side, about 5 more minutes. Take the chicken out of the pan and put it on a platter.

> Add the chopped tomatoes and the strained tomato juice to the pan, along with the vinegar. Bring to a simmer, scraping the bottom of the pan with a wooden spoon to pull up the brown bits. Return the chicken to the pan along with any juices that have accumulated on the plate. Nestle the dark meat pieces under the sauce, as they take the longest to cook. Bring to a simmer over low heat and cook uncovered until the chicken is cooked through, about 20 minutes.

> Remove the chicken to a serving platter. Simmer the sauce to reduce and thicken, 3 to 5 minutes. Stir in the basil, the remaining $1/2$ teaspoon salt, and the olives. Return the chicken to the pan and cook for 2 minutes over very low heat to marry the flavors. Serve hot with good bread.

Grilled spatchcocked chicken with moroccan spices

Butterflying (a.k.a. "spatchcocking") is a great way to prepare a whole chicken that produces a fabulously crisp skin, and it cooks faster than your standard whole chicken: The backbone is cut out and the breastbone split so that the bird can lie flat. The recipe below gives directions for butterflying, and it's not particularly hard—but in a pinch, you should be able to seduce your butcher into doing it for you.

The marinade for this is made with a few of the spices used in the Moroccan pigeon pie *bastila*: cinnamon, cumin, and ginger—spices that make the bird taste exotic. You also can't go wrong marinating the bird with whatever fresh herb you have around, along with lemon slices, garlic, and a little oil. Of *major* importance if you're going to grill chicken is that your fire be low to medium low, not hot. The skin burns quickly, and if it does, you won't be happy. If instead you want to roast the bird, brown it first, skin side down, in a couple of tablespoons of oil in a large, ovenproof sauté pan, then stick it in a 400°F. oven for 30 to 40 minutes.

SERVES 4 / WINE PAIRING: Rich Viognier from France or California

1 whole chicken (about 4 pounds)
1 teaspoon ground cinnamon
1½ teaspoons ground cumin
½ teaspoon ground ginger
¼ teaspoon freshly ground black pepper
2 tablespoons extra-virgin olive oil
1 lemon, cut into thin slices, plus 1 lemon, cut into wedges, for serving
1 small onion, sliced
2 tablespoons roughly chopped flat-leaf parsley
½ teaspoon kosher salt

> To butterfly the chicken, set it on the neck end with the breast facing away from you. Hold the left side firmly with your left hand and use a chef's knife to cut down the right side of the backbone. Then set the bird on its back, and cut down the other side of the backbone to remove it. Now put the bird on its breast and pry open the two sides of the body. Give the top (the white part) of the breastbone a whack with the knife to split it. Then press the chicken open with your hands.

> In a small bowl, combine the cinnamon, cumin, ginger, and pepper. Sprinkle the spices over the bird in a baking dish, and rub them into the chicken. Add the olive oil, lemon slices, onion, parsley, and salt and rub them into the bird, too. Then cover and refrigerate for a while (overnight, if you can).

> Build a fire in a charcoal or gas grill. You're going to grill the chicken over indirect heat, so build a two-level fire, if you have a charcoal grill. Or heat a gas grill and then turn half the burners off. Put the chicken on the grill skin side down and grill until the skin is lightly browned and crisp. (Watch carefully for flare-ups and move the chicken around or adjust your fire or heat as needed.) Optimally, you want the skin to brown slowly and evenly so that it's perfect after about 20 minutes. Then turn the bird and continue cooking until the juices run clear, 35 to 40 minutes total. Remove to a platter and cut into pieces. Squeeze the lemon wedges over and serve.

Around the world on a chicken breast—or something

Boneless, skinless chicken breasts are practical, quick-cooking dinner items (and the diet crowd likes them) but they also have little in the way of flavor. Actually, they're boring. Fortunately, that makes them excellent "canvases," if you will: blank slates that are superb vehicles for other great flavors.

Thai green chicken curry with vegetables

A traditional Thai curry is flavored with kaffir lime leaves (a brilliant, subtle ingredient) and fish sauce (a very *un*subtle ingredient). In the right combinations, though, these flavors can be amazing. Fish sauce is widely available at grocery stores, but kaffir lime leaves definitely are not—that's going to take a trip to an Asian market. In case you're not up for a special trip, lime zest and juice make a reasonable substitute for the leaves, and soy sauce is a passable swap (if not nearly assertive enough) for the fish sauce. Serve over rice (see Notes).

SERVES 4 / WINE PAIRING: Fruity Gamay

2 tablespoons plus 1 teaspoon canola oil

1 medium onion, sliced (about 2 cups)

1 medium red bell pepper, stemmed, seeded, and cut lengthwise 1 inch thick

$3/4$ pound snow peas

$1/2$ pound shiitake mushrooms, stemmed and sliced

$1/2$ teaspoon kosher salt, plus more to taste

2 teaspoons grated fresh ginger

2 large garlic cloves, chopped (about 1 tablespoon)

1 stalk lemongrass, white bulb only (the bottom 3 inches), trimmed and smashed
      with the side of a large knife

1 can (14 ounces) coconut milk

1 tablespoon Thai green curry paste (see Note)

$1^1/2$ pounds boneless, skinless chicken breast, sliced crosswise about
      $1/4$ inch thick

10 kaffir lime leaves, or substitute grated zest (about 1 teaspoon) and juice
      (about $1/4$ cup) of 2 limes

1 tablespoon fish sauce or soy sauce

$1/4$ cup chopped fresh cilantro

2 tablespoons torn basil leaves (10 to 12 leaves)

> Heat 2 tablespoons of the canola oil in a wok or large, deep frying pan over a medium-high flame until smoking. Add the onion, red pepper, snow peas, mushrooms, and $1/2$ teaspoon salt and cook, stirring, for 4 minutes, or until the vegetables are softened. Remove to a bowl with a slotted spoon, leaving whatever oil remains in the wok or frying pan.

> Now add the remaining 1 teaspoon of oil to the pan. Add the ginger, garlic, and lemongrass and cook for 1 minute, stirring, over medium-low heat, until fragrant but not browned. Add about one quarter of the can of coconut milk and the curry paste and stir to dissolve the paste. Then add the chicken, the reserved vegetables, and salt to taste. Raise the heat to medium high and cook, stirring, until the chicken is no longer pink, about 3 minutes. Add the remaining coconut milk, the lime leaves (or zest and juice), and the fish sauce or soy sauce. Bring to a simmer, reduce the heat to low, and cook for 1 minute to marry the flavors and thoroughly cook the chicken. Stir in the chopped herbs. Taste for salt and serve.

NOTES: Thai curry pastes (red and green)—pounded or puréed mixtures of garlic, herbs, and chilies—are available in any well-stocked Asian aisle of your supermarket in little glass bottles, next to the coconut milk. The red and the green have slightly different flavors; both are very, very spicy.

To make basic white rice: In a medium saucepan with a tight-fitting lid, combine 1 cup rice, 1½ cups water, and 1 teaspoon salt. Bring to a boil, then reduce the heat to the barest simmer, cover, and let cook—without peeking under the cover—for 15 minutes. Turn off the heat and let sit for 5 minutes. Uncover, fluff with a fork, and serve.

Tandoori (ish) chicken

Marinated in spiced yogurt, this chicken gets very tender with a moist coating. It's spicy, but not terribly hot; you can make it hotter by adding more cayenne. The name comes from the free-standing, cylindrical, wood-fired clay oven called the tandoor, which you may have seen in Indian restaurants. Food is placed on long skewers and lowered into the heat. Chances are quite good that you don't own a tandoor, but you can approximate its fantastic, charred crustiness on a regular grill.

SERVES 4 / WINE PAIRING: Riesling Kabinett or Alsatian Gewürztztraminer

for the marinade

$^1/_2$ medium onion, quartered

3 medium garlic cloves

2-inch piece of fresh ginger, peeled

Juice of $^1/_2$ lemon (about 1 tablespoon)

$^1/_2$ cup plain yogurt

1 teaspoon kosher salt

$^1/_2$ teaspoon ground cumin

$^1/_4$ teaspoon ground turmeric

$^1/_4$ teaspoon ground cinnamon

$^1/_4$ teaspoon freshly ground black pepper

Pinch of cayenne pepper

Pinch of ground cardamom

for the chicken

$1^1/_2$ to 2 pounds boneless, skinless chicken breasts, cut crosswise
$1^1/_2$ to 2 inches thick

3 tablespoons all-purpose flour

2 tablespoons vegetable oil

1 lemon or lime cut into wedges, for serving

> Combine all of the marinade ingredients in a blender and purée. Pour out into a glass baking dish. Add the chicken and stir to coat. Add the flour and stir to combine. Cover and refrigerate for at least 2 hours or overnight.

> Preheat a charcoal or gas grill. Just before you're ready to cook, add the oil to the chicken mixture and stir (this will keep the chicken from sticking to the grill). Also, before you put your grate over the coals, lightly oil it, too, with several folded paper towels drizzled with oil. Then, heat up the grate for a few minutes, check to see that the coals have reached medium-high heat (when you can hold your hand 5 inches above the grate for only 3 seconds), and place the chicken on the grill. Cook until browned on each side, 8 to 10 minutes total. Serve with Cucumber Yogurt Dip (page 24) and lemon or lime wedges.

Chicken parmigiana

This red-sauce classic has always been a favorite of mine, and it's a crowd pleaser—just break out a loaf of crusty bread and a green salad with a tart vinaigrette to lighten up the richness of the entrée. Sautéeing breaded chicken on the stovetop gets you a nice crust; then, you finish the breasts in the oven with that lush marinara.

SERVES 4 / WINE PAIRING: Full-bodied Montepulciano

4 slices of white bread (stale is good, if you have it)

1 tablespoon chopped flat-leaf parsley

1 tablespoon chopped fresh basil, or 1 teaspoon thyme or oregano leaves (optional)

$3/4$ cup freshly grated Parmigiano-Reggiano

$1/2$ cup all-purpose flour

1 teaspoon plus 1 pinch kosher salt

$1/2$ teaspoon plus 2 pinches freshly ground black pepper

1 large egg

$1/4$ cup extra-virgin olive oil

4 boneless, skinless chicken breasts ($1^{1}/2$ to $1^{3}/4$ pounds total)

1 recipe Basic Tomato Sauce (page 66)

8 ounces mozzarella cheese, sliced

> Put the bread in the food processor and process into crumbs. Dump out onto a large plate. Stir in the chopped parsley and basil, if using, and $1/4$ cup of the Parmigiano, and season with a pinch of pepper. Measure the flour onto a second plate and season with 1 teaspoon salt and $1/2$ teaspoon pepper. Break the egg into a deep plate or shallow bowl, season with a pinch each of salt and pepper, and beat lightly with a fork to break it up. Arrange the plates in a row on your work surface near the stove: first the flour, then the egg, and finally the bread crumbs.

> Preheat the oven to 400°F. Heat the oil in a large ovenproof skillet over a medium-high flame.

> The secret to breading is to use one hand for the egg *only*, and the other hand for the flour and bread crumbs. That way you don't get both hands coated with blobs of goopy bread crumbs. So, starting with one hand, lightly dredge the chicken cutlets in the seasoned flour and pat off the excess. With your other hand, dip them in the beaten egg to coat completely and let the excess drip off. Then, drop the breast in the bread crumbs and use your first (dry) hand to sprinkle crumbs over and pat them into an even coating.

> When the oil shimmers, add the cutlets and fry for 2 to 3 minutes on each side until golden and crispy. (Turn the heat down if the bread crumbs brown too fast.) You might need to turn the thicker breasts on their sides to get the breading crisp all over; lean them against one another—it will only take about 30 seconds to brown. Drain the chicken on paper towels. Wipe out the pan.

> Spoon a thin layer of tomato sauce over the bottom of the pan. Put the chicken breasts back in the pan and sprinkle with the remaining $\frac{1}{2}$ cup Parmigiano. Now pour the rest of the tomato sauce over the chicken, and cover with the sliced mozzarella. Bake until the sauce is hot, the cheese is melted, and the chicken is cooked through, 12 to 15 minutes.

+ *VARIATION:* Chicken Milanese

Make sure your chicken breasts are thin-either because you bought them as thin cutlets, or because you sliced thicker ones in half and pounded them thin (you can use a meat tenderizer or the side of a cleaver, or anything flat and heavy that you've wrapped in plastic). Follow the recipe above through the sautéing, making sure the cutlets are cooked all the way through. Then just go ahead and serve them, with lemon wedges to squeeze over and, to round out the plate, a very simple salad of arugula tossed with Balsamic Vinaigrette (page 52).

Duck breast with a balsamic glaze

Roasting a whole duck is a bit of an undertaking because of the prodigious amount of fat that melts off and makes a mess, but duck breast is easy. You cook it just as you would a steak—that is, medium rare—and a simple pan sauce suffices for serving. Duck breast may be the easiest thing on the planet to cook, and it's delicious; balsamic vinegar reduced until it gets a little thick and sweet cuts the fattiness of the skin nicely. The dish is so simple and chic you'll feel confident serving it at the most upscale affair. Duck breast is also excellent grilled over medium heat to render as much of the fat from the skin as possible.

SERVES 4 / WINE PAIRING: Fruity Côtes du Rhône or Shiraz

1/2 teaspoon plus 1 pinch kosher salt
1/4 teaspoon plus 1 pinch freshly ground black pepper
4 duck breasts (1 1/2 to 1 3/4 pounds total)
1/2 cup balsamic vinegar

> Heat a large frying pan over a medium flame. In a small bowl, stir together 1/2 teaspoon salt and 1/4 teaspoon pepper. Lay the duck breasts on a cutting board and use a paring knife to make diagonal slashes through the skin (do not pierce the flesh) every 1/2 inch or so. Sprinkle both sides with the seasoning mixture. Put the duck breasts into the hot pan, skin side down (you'll get some dramatic sound effects when the skin hits the hot pan), and cook until the fat is rendered and the skin is browned, 5 to 7 minutes. Use a splatter screen if you have one because the breasts render a lot of fat. About halfway through the cooking, use a ladle or baster to remove most of the fat.

> Turn the breasts and cook to barely medium rare, 8 to 10 minutes total. (Lift the tenderloin—the long, skinny piece of meat attached to the breast—to check doneness; the breast is done when you can't see raw meat there anymore.) Remove the breasts to 4 serving plates or a platter and arrange them skin side up. Discard most of the fat in the pan. Then add the vinegar and cook until reduced by about half and thickened, 1 to 2 minutes. Season with a pinch each of salt and pepper. Spoon the vinegar over the breasts and serve immediately.

Roast turkey breast with warm apple chutney

A whole turkey is a lot of trouble—worth it for the holidays, probably not for Tuesday-night supper. But cooking a turkey *breast* is easy any time. And here's a trick to make it perfect: soak your turkey breast in water, salt, sugar, and seasonings, a technique called brining that has become as popular with home cooks as it's been with pro-fessionals for years. When you brine meat (it also works beautifully with chicken, pork, and other meats, too), the salt permeates the flesh, tenderizing it, seasoning it with flavor, and allowing it to retain more juices. It requires a large pot—a 4- to 6-quart pot will easily hold your average turkey breast—and a little bit of advance work the day before. But it's really easy. You and your guests will be grateful at dinnertime.

For a little extra punch, I've thrown in a chutney that marries sweet and savory flavors—a great complement in the same way cranberry sauce is, with a warm, spicy twist.

SERVES 6 WITH LEFTOVERS / WINE PAIRING: Riesling, or Cabernet Franc from Italy or the Loire Valley

for the brine

- ½ cup kosher salt
- ½ cup honey
- 1 head of garlic, cut in half
- 2 bay leaves
- 4 sprigs of fresh thyme
- 2 teaspoons black peppercorns
- 2 teaspoons allspice berries
- ¼ cup fresh celery leaves
- ½ cup white wine

for the turkey

- 1 turkey breast on the bone, 5 to 6 pounds
- 2 tablespoons unsalted butter, melted

for the chutney

- 1 tablespoon extra-virgin olive oil
- 1 medium garlic clove, sliced
- ½-inch piece of fresh ginger, peeled and thinly sliced into coins and then into thin strips (about 1 tablespoon strips)
- 1 small red onion, sliced
- ½ teaspoon kosher salt
- 2 Granny Smith apples, peeled, cored, and quartered; each quarter cut into 6 chunks

1 tablespoon sugar

2 tablespoons cider vinegar

$1/8$ teaspoon ground cumin

Pinch of ground cinnamon

Pinch of ground cloves

$1/3$ cup dried cranberries

Pinch of cayenne pepper, or more if you like spicy food

$1/3$ cup chopped fresh cilantro

> For the brine: In a saucepan, combine the $1/2$ cup salt, honey, garlic, bay leaves, thyme, peppercorns, and allspice. Add about 1 cup of water (enough to cover the salt and come about halfway up the garlic halves) and bring to a simmer to dissolve the salt. Refrigerate for about 30 minutes with ice cubes to cool it off.

> Put the turkey in a large, deep pot that will hold it snug, with enough room for the brine to cover. Pour over the chilled mixture. Add the celery leaves and the wine. Then add enough cold water to cover the turkey. Cover and refrigerate overnight.

> Preheat the oven to 400°F.

> Remove the turkey from the brine and pat dry. Line a roasting pan with aluminum foil. Set the breast, skin side up, in a V-rack (see Note, page 000) in the roasting pan and drizzle or brush with the butter. Roast until the turkey registers 160°F. on an instant-read thermometer, 1 to $1^{1}/4$ hours total for a breast weighing 5 to $5^{1}/4$ pounds, $1^{1}/2$ hours or more for a larger bird. Cover with aluminum foil if the top starts to brown too much. Remove from the oven and let stand about 10 minutes before slicing.

> While the turkey cooks, make the chutney. Heat the oil in a saucepan over a medium-low flame. Add the garlic, ginger, onion, and $1/4$ teaspoon of the salt and cook until the onion is softened, 4 to 5 minutes. Add the apples, sugar, vinegar, cumin, cinnamon, cloves, and remaining $1/4$ teaspoon of salt; cover and cook until the apples are soft, about 8 minutes. There should still be liquid in the pan. Add the cranberries and cayenne, and cook until the liquid has evaporated, 2 to 3 minutes. Transfer to a bowl and stir in the cilantro.

> Serve the sliced turkey breast with a drizzle of the juices and the warm or room-temperature chutney.

7 / Meats

Meat, so they say, is what's for dinner. Not always, of course. But it's true that for many people nothing looks quite as perfect in the center of the table as a big hunk of perfectly seasoned roasted meat with a deliciously charred crust. This chapter is about the American entrée at its most basic—but with a few twists to keep things interesting and contemporary. And it runs the gamut from the most modest of comfort foods—you need a great meat loaf and a chunky, killer chili—to the most elegant item ever to headline a dinner party, rack of lamb. Pork tenderloin has become a staple in our house—quick, delicious, versatile, and tender, not to mention much less expensive than beef tenderloin. And beef stews and pot roasts are often the perfect answer for delectable one-dish dinners.

Many of the recipes in this chapter are for stews—meat cooked slowly in a liquid such as wine, stock, water, or beer, sometimes flavored with vegetables until very tender. Even chili is essentially a beef stew flavored with ground and fresh chilies (and beans, at least when I'm cooking it—apologies to Texas). Stews usually call for cuts of meat that have lots of flavor but also a lot of tough connective tissue—and that, as such, are much less expensive than their cousins in the steak department. But when cooked low and slow, that connective tissue breaks down and you're left with a different kind of tenderness. You actually don't *want* to stew an expensive cut like filet mignon; it doesn't have enough fat to provide any flavor, and it will quickly turn to mush in these preparations.

All stews taste better the next day after a night in the refrigerator. The resting period gives the flavors a chance to mellow while the meat soaks up the taste of the sauce and vice versa. And all of the vegetables for these things can be chopped in the food processor, which will cut your work time in half.

Roast prime rib with a mustard—herb crust

This roast is coated with a simple herby, garlicky paste to add flavor to the meat (and to make your entire house smell *fabulous*). But you can just as well rub the meat with salt and freshly ground pepper and stick it in the oven like that. Ask your butcher to cut the roast from what they call "the small end," where you'll get the largest, most tender piece of meat. (You do have a butcher, right? See "The Chopping Block," opposite.) Have him remove the chine bone and cut between the ribs to make carving easier.

Serving roast prime rib is also an excellent excuse for making Yorkshire Pudding. Prepare the batter while the roast cooks, and refrigerate it. Then, while the roast is resting, you'll have the oven free to bake the pudding.

SERVES 6 / WINE PAIRING: Syrah, Rhône, or young Barolo

1 (3-rib) rib roast, 6 to 7 pounds, chine bone removed
4 large garlic cloves, coarsely chopped
3/4 teaspoon kosher salt
1/4 cup fresh rosemary needles, chopped
1/4 teaspoon freshly ground black pepper
1 tablespoon Dijon mustard
2 teaspoons balsamic vinegar
2 tablespoons extra-virgin olive oil

> Preheat the oven to 450°F.

> Place the roast in a large roasting pan with the bones facing down. On a cutting board, use a fork to mash the garlic with the salt to make a paste. Put that in a small bowl and stir in the rosemary, pepper, mustard, vinegar, and oil. Smear that all over the meaty part of the roast (not the bones). Then put the pan in the oven and roast for 15 minutes. Turn the heat down to 350°F. and continue roasting until the meat registers 125° to 130°F. (for rare meat) on an instant-read thermometer. This could take about 1 more hour for a 6-pound roast, or 1 hour and 20 minutes for a 7-pounder. (For medium rare, roast for an additional 10 minutes.)

> Remove from the oven and let stand at least 10 minutes. Lay the roast on its side (bones to one side, meaty section to the other) on a cutting board, preferably one that has an indented "gutter" around the edges for catching the juices. Holding the roast steady with a large fork, and cutting parallel to the cutting board with a large knife, cut the roast into slices. Figure on getting 2 slices from each rib—one with a bone and one without. Carve and serve with the juices and Yorkshire Pudding (recipe follows).

+ *VARIATION:* Spiced Prime Rib
Sprinkle the meat all over with about half of the recipe for Barbecue Rub on page 86 instead of the mustard glaze, and roast as in the recipe above.

Yorkshire pudding

Yorkshire Pudding is a delicious English classic—the perfect side to prime rib. It's really just a big popover that you make with a tiny bit of flavorful juices and fat from a roast (no need to tell your date about that latter ingredient). If you can get organized ahead of time, an easy way to make this batter is to combine all the ingredients except the juices in a blender and blend until smooth; let that sit in the refrigerator for at least 30 minutes before adding the juices and baking.

SERVES 6

4 large eggs
1 cup whole milk
3/4 cup all-purpose flour
3/4 teaspoon kosher salt
4 tablespoons beef fat from a roast

> In a large bowl, whisk the eggs with the milk and 1/4 cup water until frothy. Add the flour and salt and whisk just to combine. When the roast is finished cooking, take it out of the oven and let it rest. Raise the oven temperature to 500°F. Put the beef fat into a large (at least 13-inch) cast-iron pan and put it back in the oven to heat for 5 minutes. Then pour the batter into the pan and bake for 8 minutes. Reduce the heat to 400°F. and cook until the pudding is puffed and browned, 10 more minutes.

✳ The chopping block

You do have a butcher, right? If you don't, get one. Making a special trip for meats is worth it. You get fresher, higher-quality steaks and chops, you can place custom orders for particularly hard-to-find items, and you can get things cut exactly the way you want them (grocery stores have a terrible habit of selling steaks precut to a scrawny 3/4 inch). At holiday times, you can order a fresh, never-frozen turkey, which tastes markedly better than the garden-variety ones at the supermarket. Plus, you'll get service from people who know how to cook. Those guys at the supermarket meat counter just don't have the training and experience—or, usually, the passion for great food—that you'll find in a real butcher.

Pan-roasted steak

As much as I love grilling beef over genuine, red-hot charcoal, I have to admit that pan roasting produces one helluva crust—particularly if you cook the steak in butter. So here's a recipe for when your grill is out of commission, or for those of us confined to the great indoors. If you're making porterhouse, you'll need to use one pan per steak. They're huge. By the way, it's crucial to have a good range hood that vents outside with this technique; otherwise, it will make your house awfully smoky. Serve with Mashed Potatoes (page 165).

SERVES 4 / WINE PAIRING: Full-bodied Bordeaux or California Zinfandel

2 tablespoons extra-virgin olive oil

$3/4$ teaspoon kosher salt

$1/4$ teaspoon freshly ground black pepper

4 best-quality strip, T-bone, or rib-eye steaks, or 2 porterhouse steaks, about
    $1^1/_2$ inches thick

2 tablespoons unsalted butter

> Heat 2 heavy-bottomed frying pans (cast-iron, if you have them) over a medium-high flame. After at least 5 minutes, when they're good and hot, add 1 tablespoon oil to each. In a small bowl, stir together the salt and pepper. Lay the steaks on a cutting board and sprinkle on both sides with the seasoning. Put the steaks in the pans. Cook for 2 minutes, then add the butter—1 tablespoon per pan—and keep cooking until the steaks are brown on one side, 2 to 4 minutes more. Turn the steaks and continue cooking, basting with the pan juices every now and then with a long-handled spoon, until well browned on both sides, 8 to 10 minutes total for medium rare. Turn down the heat if the meat browns too fast; turn it up if it doesn't brown fast enough. If you like your steak more done, turn the heat down to medium low and keep cooking for 2 to 4 minutes.

> Remove the steaks to a platter and let them stand for 5 minutes before serving. This allows the juices to settle back into the meat.

> Want to make them a little more special? See Power Butters on page 136.

Power butters!

Ask any professional chef: Even in this diet-obsessed culture, butter is probably the single most important ingredient in the cook's arsenal. Sure, too much of it will kill you. So will too much yoga.

Here's a really easy way to make butter even better. Chefs call it *compound butter;* me, I like to say Power Butter. Take a high-quality, unsalted butter (unsalted because *you* want to control how salty your food is) and season it with something or other—herbs, garlic, lemon juice, chilies. It is an incredibly easy, effective way to add flavor to virtually anything on the table, a simple method of saucing something you've grilled or sautéed.

So for instance: You want to flavor your steak or fish fillet with an herb—say, rosemary. If you coat the meat with rosemary paste before you cook it, it might burn on the grill or in the hot pan, and you'll end up with a charred herb taste. On the other hand, you can stir some chopped rosemary into softened butter and add a little salt, pepper, and lemon juice to brighten the flavors—put a dollop of *that* on your grilled steak or fish right before you serve it. Voilà! You have a rosemary-infused entrée.

Below are just a few ideas for flavored butters. For all of them, the technique is the same: Stir everything together in a bowl and then taste it to see if it needs more salt, pepper, or lemon juice. Use the butter immediately, or dump it out onto a piece of wax paper or plastic wrap and shape and roll it into a cylinder, $1^1/2$ inches in diameter. Put the butter in the freezer; then, whenever you need some bright, fresh flavor, cut off slices as needed. The herb and porcini butters also make super-quick, dynamite pasta sauces: Cook the pasta; toss it with a little butter; sprinkle with grated Pecorino Romano or Parmigiano-Reggiano cheese, salt, and pepper; and you're done.

garlic butter

4 ounces (1 stick) unsalted butter, softened
2 medium garlic cloves mashed with $1/4$ teaspoon kosher salt
$1/8$ teaspoon freshly ground black pepper
1 teaspoon fresh lemon juice (juice of $1/2$ small lemon)

fresh herb butter

4 ounces (1 stick) unsalted butter, softened
1 tablespoon chopped fresh soft herbs such as flat-leaf parsley, basil, chervil,
   tarragon, and/or chives, or 2 teaspoons chopped fresh woody herbs such as
   thyme, rosemary, or marjoram
$1/4$ teaspoon kosher salt
$1/8$ teaspoon freshly ground black pepper
1 teaspoon fresh lemon juice (juice of $1/2$ small lemon)

porcini butter

Your supermarket might carry dried porcini mushrooms among other varieties of dried mushrooms; if not, any gourmet store will. In a clean coffee grinder, process 3 or 4 to a powder (or just chop fine), then measure; grind more if needed.

4 ounces (1 stick) unsalted butter, softened
2 tablespoons ground, dried porcini mushrooms
3/4 teaspoon kosher salt
1/8 teaspoon freshly ground black pepper
1 teaspoon fresh lemon juice (juice of 1/2 small lemon)

chipotle butter

The spicy, smoky taste of chipotle peppers is more popular than ever in American cooking; there's even a chipotle-flavored Tabasco sauce now. Chipotles are jalapeño peppers that have been smoked and canned in a Mexican barbecue sauce called adobo. Check the Mexican food section of your market.

4 ounces (1 stick) unsalted butter, softened
1 medium chipotle chili (from the can, packed in adobo sauce), cut in half, seeds scraped out, chili minced
1 teaspoon adobo sauce from the can of chipotle chilies (add more if you want real heat)
1/2 teaspoon kosher salt
1 teaspoon fresh lime juice (from 1/2 lime)

blue cheese steak topping

Talk about gilding the sirloin. I like the unctuous, salty tang of Maytag blue cheese (developed in Iowa by Fred Maytag II of appliance fame!), but you can substitute any blue cheese such as French Roquefort or Italian Gorgonzola, or switch to a Greek feta.

MAKES ABOUT 1/2 CUP OR ENOUGH FOR 4 STEAKS

1/2 teaspoon black peppercorns
1/2 cup crumbled Maytag or other blue cheese
1 tablespoon chopped flat-leaf parsley

> Crack the peppercorns with a mortar and pestle. Or put the peppercorns in a resealable plastic freezer bag and put the bag on a cutting board. Then whack it several times with a rolling pin until the peppercorns are coarsely cracked (not finely ground). Put the cracked pepper in a bowl, add the cheese and parsley, and stir together gently with a fork, just to combine. Serve on hot steak.

Pot roast with parsnips and horseradish

Horseradish and parsnips number among my favorite foods and they also happen to taste good together. There are a number of great cuts of beef suitable for pot roast, including the brisket I've used here. You might also try any boneless hunk of meat cut from the chuck (shoulder) such as a top blade roast. But don't buy roast cuts from the round (the leg) such as top round or bottom round; these are leaner than shoulder cuts and make a dry pot roast. The leftovers here are great in Mom's Vegetable Beef Soup (page 148).

SERVES 4 WITH LEFTOVERS / WINE PAIRING: Cabernet Franc or Shiraz

1 3- to 3 $\frac{1}{2}$-pound brisket, cut in half crosswise to make it more manageable

1$\frac{1}{2}$ teaspoons kosher salt

2 tablespoons extra-virgin olive oil

2 medium onions, chopped

2 cups canned low-sodium chicken stock

6 garlic cloves, smashed with the flat side of a large knife

2 bay leaves

1$\frac{1}{2}$ teaspoons dried thyme

1 teaspoon fennel seed

$\frac{1}{4}$ cup prepared horseradish, squeezed dry, plus plenty of extra for serving

3 medium carrots, peeled, skinny ends cut 1 inch long, wide ends halved or quartered and sliced 1 inch thick

2 celery stalks, cut into 1 $\frac{1}{2}$-inch pieces

$\frac{1}{2}$ pound parsnips, peeled, skinny ends cut 1 inch long, wide ends halved or quartered and sliced $\frac{1}{2}$ inch thick

Coarse sea salt, for serving

> Preheat the oven to 350°F.

> Put a heavy-bottomed pot or Dutch oven over high heat and let it sit there for 4 minutes until it gets very hot. Meanwhile, sprinkle the brisket on both sides with 1$\frac{1}{2}$ teaspoons salt. When the pot is hot, add the oil. Then add one of the brisket halves, fat side down, and cook until browned on both sides, about 5 minutes total. Remove to a plate. Put the other half of the brisket in the pot and brown the same way. Remove to the plate as well.

> Add the onions to the pot and turn the heat down to medium high. Cook, scraping the bottom of the pot with a wooden spoon to pick up all of the brown bits, until the onions are good and brown, about 10 minutes. Then add the stock; it will turn a lovely dark brown color as well. Add the garlic, bay leaves, thyme, fennel, and the $\frac{1}{4}$ cup horseradish.

> Put the meat back in the pan and bring the stock to a simmer. Cover the pot and put it on the bottom rack of the oven. Bake for 2¼ hours. Add the carrots, celery, and parsnips, tucking the vegetables under the beef, and continue baking until the vegetables are tender and the brisket can be cut with a fork, about 3 hours total.

> When it is cooked, transfer the brisket to a cutting board and cut into thick slices across the grain of the meat. (You'll see that the meat pulls apart in strands, all of which run in the same direction. Those strands are delicious but chewy. Cut perpendicular to the strands so that the knife does part of your chewing for you; that's what it means to cut against the grain.) Serve the meat with the vegetables, broth, coarse salt, and plenty of horseradish on the side.

Beef tenderloin with black pepper and horseradish

If you're cooking for a love interest who loves beef, here's the ultimate, special-occasion entrée—you can't go wrong. (Unless you overcook it. Please don't.) It's also great if your boss is coming over for dinner. Beef tenderloin is expensive, but people love it—and here's the kicker: It's one of the easiest entrées you'll ever prepare. You can do a whole tenderloin if you like, but you'll need a gigantic roasting pan to do so—a tenderloin weighs 4½ to 5 pounds, and even with the skinny tail end folded under, it's still a good foot and a half long. Plus, that will break the bank and feed an army. A 3-pound tenderloin gives you enough meat to serve 4 people comfortably with about a pound left over for sandwiches, and you can cook it in an ordinary roasting pan.

I like to brown tenderloin on top of the stove before roasting; tenderloin cooks so quickly and it's so lean that it won't develop any of that lovely crustiness if you don't.

SERVES 4 WITH LEFTOVERS / WINE PAIRING: Full-bodied Gavi

for the beef

Scant ¼ cup black peppercorns

3 pounds beef tenderloin, tied every 2 to 3 inches to hold its shape (ask your butcher to do this for you)

1 teaspoon kosher salt

2 tablespoons extra-virgin olive oil

2 tablespoons unsalted butter

Coarse sea salt, for serving (optional)

for the horseradish cream

½ cup sour cream or crème fraîche

2 tablespoons freshly grated, or well-drained jarred, horseradish

1 tablespoon fresh lemon juice (from ½ lemon)

1 tablespoon chopped flat-leaf parsley (optional)

¼ teaspoon kosher salt

> Preheat the oven to 425°F. Crack the peppercorns with a mortar and pestle. Or put them in a resealable plastic freezer bag and place the bag on a cutting board so that the peppercorns are in a single layer. Pound with a rolling pin until you've got a nice coarsely cracked texture. Spread the peppercorns over a large plate or platter and press the beef in them to coat. Sprinkle all over with the 1 teaspoon salt.

> Heat a roasting pan large enough to hold the meat comfortably over two burners on medium-high flames. When the pan is hot, add the oil and butter to coat the bottom of the pan. Put the tenderloin in the pan and brown all over, 5 to 6 minutes. Put the pan in the oven and roast until the meat registers 120°F. on an instant-read thermometer, about 20 minutes, for rare, another 4 or 5 minutes for medium. Let rest for 10 minutes.

> Meanwhile, in a small bowl, stir together the sour cream or crème fraîche, horse-radish, lemon juice, and parsley, if using. Season with the 1/4 teaspoon salt.

> Cut the beef into 3/4-inch-thick slices and arrange on a warm platter. Serve with the horseradish sauce and coarse sea salt, if using.

✳ Internal temperatures for beef roasts

Meat continues to cook *after* you take it out of the oven, particularly when you're roasting large cuts. So without a lot of experience, it's tough to gauge when it's done. The best way to get a feel for roasting is to get yourself an instant-read thermometer: They're cheap, they're available in any grocery or hardware store, and they're the only way to know what's happening inside that delicious roast without cutting into it and losing juices. As soon as you take the roast out of the oven, insert the thermometer until its tip reaches the thickest part of the meat. Then watch as the temperature continues to slowly rise.

Rare: 120° to 125°F.

Medium rare: 130° F.

Medium: 135° to 140°F.

Osso buco

This is a delicious, traditional recipe. The meat melts in your mouth, the sauce tastes luxuriously of the rich flavor of veal, and the buttery marrow from the center of the bones is prized by foodies (but you don't *have* to eat it). By chopping the vegetables in a food processor, you cut your prep time down to practically nothing. The carrots make the sauce wonderfully sweet.

Serve it with bread or throw 6 to 8 small, unskinned new potatoes into the pot before baking; entirely untraditional, but mushed into the sauce the potatoes taste great. Osso buco is traditionally served with a garnish called gremolata, a simple, aromatic combination of chopped parsley, garlic, and lemon zest.

SERVES 4 / WINE PAIRING: Aged Barolo or Aglianico

1 large onion, cut into large chunks

3 medium carrots, cut into large chunks

1 celery stalk, cut into large chunks

3 medium garlic cloves, crushed

8 large sprigs of flat-leaf parsley

4 tablespoons ($1/2$ stick) unsalted butter

3 sprigs of fresh thyme

2 bay leaves

$3/4$ teaspoon kosher salt

3 tablespoons extra-virgin olive oil

$3/4$ cup all-purpose flour

4 veal shanks, 2 inches thick, tied around the perimeter with string to keep them
   from falling apart during cooking (3 to $31/2$ pounds)

$1/4$ teaspoon freshly ground black pepper

$3/4$ cup dry white wine, such as a Pinot Grigio

1 cup canned low-sodium chicken stock or water

1 teaspoon finely minced garlic

1 teaspoon grated lemon zest

> Preheat the oven to 350°F.

> In a food processor, combine the onion, carrots, celery, and garlic, and pulse to chop. Pull the leaves off the parsley stems and chop by hand; you should have about 2 tablespoons parsley. Set the leaves aside for the gremolata, but save the stems.

> Melt the butter in a Dutch oven or wide, shallow (4 to 5 inches high) pot over medium heat. Add the chopped vegetables, thyme, bay leaves, and $1/4$ teaspoon of the salt. Cook, stirring occasionally, until the vegetables are softened but not browned, about 10 minutes.

> Meanwhile, heat the olive oil in a large frying pan over a medium-high flame until smoking. Put the flour in a large paper or plastic bag, add the veal, and shake the bag to coat the veal with the flour. Remove the veal from the bag and shake off the

excess flour. Put the veal on a plate or cutting board and sprinkle with the remaining $1/2$ teaspoon of salt and the pepper. When the oil is hot, put the veal in the pan and cook until well browned on one side, 3 to 4 minutes. Then turn and brown on the other side. Move the browned veal to the pot with the vegetables. Discard the fat from the frying pan. Add the wine to the pan and cook, scraping the bottom of the pan with a wooden spoon to pick up any browned bits, for 1 minute. Pour that into the pot with the veal and vegetables, then add the stock and reserved parsley stems. Bring to a boil, cover, and put the pot in the oven. Braise until the veal is very tender and falling off the bone, $1^3/4$ to 2 hours.

> While the meat cooks, make the gremolata: stir together the reserved 2 table-spoons chopped parsley, the minced garlic, and the lemon zest. Set aside.

> When the meat is tender, remove it to a deep serving platter. Put the pot over medium-high heat and reduce until the liquid is just thick enough to coat the back of a spoon, about 5 minutes. The sauce shouldn't be thick, but rather thickened juices with lots of vegetables. Remove the parsley stems, thyme sprigs, and bay leaves. Pour the sauce over the veal and sprinkle with the gremolata. Serve hot.

Meat loaf

A combination of ground pork and beef gives meat loaf a more interesting flavor than beef alone. Make sure to get dark brown *toasted* walnut oil for the mushroom sauce (you'll find it at a gourmet store — look for a French brand). Toasted walnut oil has a sweet, warm taste that picks up the woodsy flavor of the mushrooms. Serve with Mashed Potatoes (page 165) for a whole comfort-food extravaganza.

SERVES 4 TO 6 / WINE PAIRING: Petit Syrah, California Cabernet Sauvignon, or Valpolicella

for the meat loaf

1 cup firmly packed torn 1/2-inch pieces of good-quality white bread (2 to 3 slices)

1 cup whole milk

1 medium onion, chopped

1 1/2 pounds ground beef chuck

1/2 pound ground pork

2 large eggs

2 garlic cloves, minced

2 teaspoons Worcestershire sauce

1 tablespoon Dijon mustard

1 teaspoon kosher salt

1/2 teaspoon freshly ground black pepper

for the mushroom—walnut sauce

1 tablespoon extra-virgin olive oil

1 tablespoon unsalted butter

4 cups stemmed and thinly sliced portobello mushrooms (about 6 ounces)

1/2 teaspoon kosher salt

1 garlic clove, chopped

1 tablespoon all-purpose flour

1 cup canned low-sodium chicken stock

1 tablespoon chopped flat-leaf parsley

3/4 teaspoon toasted walnut oil

1/4 teaspoon freshly ground black pepper

> Preheat the oven to 350°F.

> Put the bread in a small bowl, pour the milk over, and set that aside while you make the rest of the meat loaf. Stir the bread every now and then so it gets completely soggy.

> In a large bowl, combine the onion with the ground meats, eggs, garlic, Worcestershire, mustard, 1 teaspoon salt, and 1/2 teaspoon pepper. Mix with your hands or a spoon (hands work much better) until it's all combined. Now add the bread-and-milk

mixture and gently work that into the meat until just combined. (There will be bits of bread — don't worry about it.)

> Form the meat mixture into a 9 × 5-inch loaf down the center of a 9 × 13-inch baking dish. Bake for 50 to 60 minutes, until an instant-read thermometer stuck into the center of the loaf reads 155°F. to 160°F. Take the meat loaf out of the oven and set it aside while you make the sauce.

> In a medium frying pan, heat the oil and butter over a medium-high flame. Add the mushrooms and 1/2 teaspoon salt and cook, stirring, until the mushrooms have given up their liquid, the liquid has evaporated, and the mushrooms are wilted, 4 to 5 minutes. Spoon off any juices that have accumulated in the baking dish with the meat loaf and add that to the pan for flavor; cook until the liquid has evaporated. Now stir in the garlic and cook until fragrant, about 10 seconds. Turn the heat down to low, stir in the flour, and cook for 30 seconds. Add the stock, increase the heat to medium high, and bring to a boil, stirring and scraping the bottom of the pan to pick up all the brown bits. Reduce the heat and simmer for 2 minutes. Take the pan off the heat. Stir in the parsley, walnut oil, and 1/4 teaspoon pepper.

> Cut the meat loaf into thick slices and put each slice on a plate. Spoon some of the sauce over and serve hot.

+ *VARIATION:* Meat Loaf with Parmigiano and Tomato
Add 1/2 cup grated Parmigiano-Reggiano to the meat mixture and cook as above. Serve with Basic Tomato Sauce (page 66).

✷ Warming your plates

Food stays hot longer when you serve it on warmed plates. But most of us aren't lucky enough to have a dedicated plate-warming drawer. Instead, set your oven at its lowest temperature — usually 170,F. — and leave it on for *only* 2 minutes (this varies oven by oven, so you'll have to experiment). Then turn the oven off and arrange your plates and platters on the racks. After 10 minutes or so, your plates should be nicely warmed but not so hot that you can't hold them barehanded.

Killer chili

I don't like my chili with ground beef. It's got to have big chunks of meat—meat that's been cooked enough to be tender, but that still has texture. Chuck is the best cut for this because it has a lot of meaty flavor. It needs to be cooked low and slow for a long time to tenderize it.

Now, with all apologies to Texas tradition, I also make my chili with beans. Usually black beans, but often black and red ones together. Sometimes I even use black-eyed peas. I mean, why not? I make it with whatever veggies are sitting around and that seem reasonable. (Now, Cincinatti people top their chili with spaghetti noodles—*that* is just not natural.)

Most stews taste better the next day, and this is particularly true of chili. The spices will mellow and the flavors marry if you let the chili sit at least 2 to 3 hours or overnight before serving. Needless to say, the leftovers are heaven.

I always serve chili with the classic accompaniments of chopped green onion, sharp Cheddar cheese, fresh jalapeño slices, hot sauce, lime wedges, and sour cream. Oh, and jalapeño cornbread. And salad. And beer.

SERVES 6 TO 8 / WINE PAIRING: Ripe Zinfandel or Syrah

3 pounds beef chuck roast

1½ teaspoons kosher salt

¾ teaspoon freshly ground black pepper

½ pound sliced bacon, cut crosswise into ½-inch pieces

1 medium onion, chopped

6 medium garlic cloves, chopped

2 jalapeño peppers, seeded and chopped

1 tablespoon chili powder

1 tablespoon ground ancho chili powder (see Note) or paprika

2 tablespoons ground cumin

1 tablespoon dried oregano

¼ teaspoon ground allspice (optional)

1 can (28 ounces) peeled, whole tomatoes (preferably San Marzano variety),
    with juice

1 bottle (12 ounces) medium-heft beer, such as Sierra Nevada Pale Ale

2 bay leaves

2 cans (19 ounces each) red beans, drained and rinsed

2 tablespoons cornmeal

Sour cream, for serving

2 limes, quartered, for serving

> First cut the beef into approximately 1-inch cubes. Cut out and throw away any really big hunks of fat—a little fat will make the chili taste good, but don't go over-board. And don't worry if the cubes are different sizes. (A 3-pound piece of chuck may come in a slab 1¼ inches thick, for instance, from which it will be impossible to cut 1-inch cubes.) Put the cubes on a big plate, sprinkle with the salt and pepper, and set aside.

> Put the bacon in a Dutch oven or large pot and cook over medium heat until the fat is rendered and the bacon is crisp, 6 to 7 minutes. About halfway through the cooking, use a large spoon to remove the fat into a bowl, and set aside. When the bacon is cooked, remove it to a different large bowl.

> Spoon out all but 1 tablespoon of the bacon fat from the pot and put the pot back over medium-high heat. Add about one third of the meat to the pan and cook for 5 minutes, stirring every now and then, until lightly browned. Turn the heat down if the meat begins to burn on the bottom of the pot. Turn off the heat and use the slotted spoon to remove the meat to the bowl with the bacon. Put the pot back over medium-high heat and continue in this same way, adding up to 1 tablespoon more of the reserved bacon fat per batch, to cook the meat in 2 more batches. (Don't try browning all the meat at once. There's too much of it.)

> Add 1 more tablespoon of the bacon fat to the pot and set it over low heat. Add the onion, cover, and cook for 5 minutes, stirring every now and then, until wilted. Add the garlic and jalapeños and cook uncovered for 2 more minutes, until soft.

> Meanwhile, in a small bowl, combine the chili powder, ancho chili powder or paprika, cumin, oregano, and allspice, if using. When the vegetables are cooked, add the spices to the pan along with 2 tablepoons water (the water will keep the spices from burning) and cook, stirring, for 30 seconds. Then add the tomatoes and their juice, and break the tomatoes into pieces with the side of your wooden spoon. Add the beer and bay leaves and stir. Then add 1 quart of water. Bring to a simmer and cook, partially covered, for 2 hours, or until the meat is tender. After 2 hours, stir the beans into the chili along with the cornmeal. Uncover and simmer for 30 more minutes or until the meat is very, very tender and the flavors are spectacular. Serve over rice (page 121), with the sour cream and lime wedges.

NOTE: McCormick sells a ground ancho chili powder. Ancho is a medium hot chili, so your chili will be moderately hot. Paprika adds no heat at all.

Mom's vegetable beef soup

This delicious, different-every-time soup always reminds me of Mom and Dad and lazy Sundays. It's as versatile as it gets—pretty much whatever veggies she has on hand are going into the pot—and it has two of Dad's very favorite things: roast beef and tomatoes, which is probably why she makes it so often. Whenever she braises a hunk of meat (like, for example, my short ribs, page 16; Osso Buco, page 142; or Pot Roast, page 138), she saves whatever meat, gravies, and broths are left over and freezes them in plastic quart containers. Then, when she has a bunch of stuff in the freezer, she puts it all together into a big pot with canned tomatoes, fresh vegetables, and cooked starches—and it's fantastic. Leftover rice from yesterday's takeout? Into the pot. Extra egg noodles? Same deal. If you don't have enough broth or gravy, supplement with canned stock.

This gets even better the longer it sits in your refrigerator, until about 4 days, at which point you have to toss it—so eat, already, Mom might say.

FEEDS A SMALL ARMY / WINE PAIRING: Sparkling Wine or Fruity Barbera

2 large onions, chopped

10 cups beef, veal, or chicken stock with whatever bits of meat you have on hand

3 cans (28 ounces) diced tomatoes

1 can (15 ounces) sliced, cooked okra

1 1-pound bag frozen mixed vegetables (must contain green beans)

1/2 head of green or Savoy cabbage, halved, cored, and chopped

1 to 2 cups whatever cooked vegetables, rice or noodles, or herbs you have on hand

Kosher salt and freshly ground black pepper, to taste

Hot sauce, for serving

> Put everything into a large stockpot, cover, and simmer for 30 minutes, or until the cabbage is tender and the flavors have blended. Taste for seasoning and add salt and pepper as needed. Ladle into bowls and add a few drops of hot sauce.

Roasted pork shoulder pernil

A traditional Puerto Rican dish, perfect for a big Sunday supper with company. It was originally done with an entire suckling pig, but that's a lot to manage in an average-size oven, so most folks these days use pork shoulder. This fabulous cut of pork has a lot of connective tissue that softens deliciously as it cooks, so the meat becomes luscious and tender with long cooking. It's also hard to ruin this cut — it just keeps getting more tender, unless you overcook it by a matter of hours. With these aromas in your house, you'll be too hungry to do that. The grilled corn on page 161 is the perfect side dish.

SERVES 6 TO 8 / WINE PAIRING: Italian Nebbiolo

6 medium garlic cloves
1/4 cup loosely packed fresh oregano leaves
2 tablespoons extra-virgin olive oil
2 tablespoons kosher salt
2 teaspoons coarsely ground black pepper
1 pork shoulder, with bone and fat (6 to 7 pounds)
3 tablespoons cider vinegar, or red or white wine vinegar

> In a food processor, combine the garlic and oregano and process to chop. Scrape out into a large bowl, add the oil, salt, and pepper, and stir to combine. With a paring knife, cut several slits all over the pork. Then rub the garlic mixture all over the pork, massaging it into the meat with your hands and poking the mix into the cuts to flavor the meat throughout. Put the pork in a resealable plastic bag (a 1-gallon freezer bag will work), add the vinegar, seal the bag, and massage the pork in the bag to incorporate the vinegar. Put the bag in a bowl in the refrigerator and let the pork marinate overnight.

> Preheat the oven to 350°F.

> Put the pork in a small roasting pan, fatty side up, and cook until the internal temperature reaches 165°F. to 170°F., 2 1/2 to 3 hours. As the pork roasts, the fat will render; use a baster or long-handled spoon to baste the meat with the melted fat, every 45 minutes or when you remember. When fully cooked, let rest for 10 minutes. Then cut into slices and serve as is. If you'd like a sauce — albeit a non-traditional one — try the Green Herb Sauce on page 104, replacing the mint and basil with equal amounts of cilantro and flat-leaf parsley.

Grilled pork tenderloin with asian flavors

Pork tenderloin has become hugely popular at home and in restaurants in the last few years, and why not? It's easy, it's quick, it's lean, it's tender, and it's a good foil for a number of flavors. Here's an Asian version, plus a vaguely Mexican variation. Of course, you don't have to get fancy; you can simply grill a 3/4- to 1-pound tenderloin, with salt and pepper, for 10 to 13 minutes, and have a nice dinner. Or you can marinate the meat in the mustard–lemon marinade used for the Roasted Chicken Parts on page 109.

Here's an important point about cooking pork these days: It is perfectly safe (and much tastier) to serve today's pork tenderloin medium or medium rare. No one has contracted a case of trichinosis since the thirties. Serve this with My Favorite Potato Gratin (page 164).

SERVES 4 / WINE PAIRING: Loire Valley Savennieres

2 tablespoons soy sauce
2 teaspoons sake or dry sherry
1½ teaspoons honey
3/4 teaspoon toasted sesame oil
1/2 teaspoon hot chili paste or crushed red pepperflakes (optional)
2 pork tenderloins, 3/4 to 1 pound each

> In a small bowl, stir together the soy sauce, sake or sherry, honey, sesame oil, and chili paste, if using. Build a fire in a charcoal grill or preheat a gas grill (see page 85). Put the tenderloins on the grill over medium-high heat and cook for 4 minutes. Turn, and brush with the soy glaze. Cook for 4 minutes. Turn and brush again with the glaze. Pull the pork off the heat to a cooler section of the grill and continue cooking, turning and brushing every now and then with the glaze, until a good crust has developed and the pork's internal temperature has reached 140°F. (for medium, 10 to 13 minutes total). Watch the meat carefully: The glaze burns easily, and you should pull the meat off the heat if you see it burning. Let it stand for 5 minutes before slicing.

+ *VARIATION:* **Grilled Pork Tenderloin with Poblano Chili and Goat Cheese** Butterfly the tenderloins by cutting them almost in half lengthwise and opening them up like a book (it sometimes helps to use a meat pounder or the back of a cleaver to flatten the meat a little). Sprinkle half of each loin with 1/4 teaspoon salt and 1/4 teaspoon black pepper. Then sprinkle each with 2 ounces goat cheese, 1/4 teaspoon dried oregano, 2 teaspoons olive oil, and 1/8 teaspoon black pepper. Lay 1 canned, roasted poblano pepper—cut in half lengthwise—over the cheese. Fold the other side of the pork over to enclose the filling. Tie the tenderloins at 1-inch intervals with kitchen string and sprinkle each with 1/2 teaspoon salt and 1/8 teaspoon pepper. Continue as in the recipe above and serve with lime wedges.

Red-wine roast rack of lamb with roasted garlic and shallots

A beautiful, delicious special-occasion entrée—one of my very favorite dishes. Pair it with Rosemary Roasted Vegetables (page 162).

SERVES 4 / WINE PAIRING: Bordeaux from St.-Emilion, or earthy Rhône

1 head of garlic, unpeeled

4 medium shallots (about $\frac{1}{2}$ pound), unpeeled

2 tablespoons extra-virgin olive oil

1 teaspoon kosher salt, plus more to taste

2 racks of lamb, about $1\frac{1}{4}$ pounds each (7 or 8 ribs each)

$\frac{1}{2}$ teaspoon freshly ground black pepper, plus more to taste

1 cup full-bodied red wine

1 tablespoon unsalted butter, optional

> Preheat the oven to 400°F.

> Break the head of garlic into cloves, but don't peel. Cut the shallots (still unpeeled) in half through the root ends. Put the garlic and shallots in a small baking dish, drizzle with 1 tablespoon of the oil, and sprinkle with $\frac{1}{2}$ teaspoon of the salt. Toss to coat the vegetables with the oil. Put the baking dish in the oven and roast for 30 minutes, or until both garlic and shallots are tender.

> When the vegetables have cooked for 20 minutes, heat the remaining tablespoon of oil in a large ovenproof frying pan over a medium-high flame. Sprinkle the racks on both sides with the remaining $\frac{1}{2}$ teaspoon salt and the $\frac{1}{2}$ teaspoon of the pepper. When the pan is hot (the oil will shimmer and if you tilt the pan, you'll see that the oil has become thin enough to coat it easily), add one of the racks, fat side down, and cook for about 4 minutes. Turn the rack and then add the other rack to the pan, fat side down. Shove the racks around a little bit so they fit in the pan.

> Cook for another 3 to 4 minutes, until the first rack is browned all over. Brown that first rack on the bottom, too; you can stand it up in the pan, leaning it against the second rack to keep it steady. When it is good and brown, remove the first rack to a plate and continue cooking the second, turning to brown it all over. Each rack should take 7 to 8 minutes total to brown completely. Make sure that the fat in the pan doesn't burn; you need it for your sauce. If you even *suspect* that the fat is beginning to burn, turn the heat down to medium.

> By now the garlic and shallots should be done. Take them out of the oven and turn the oven temperature up to 425°F. Put both racks in the ovenproof frying pan and arrange them so that they are standing up slightly, leaning toward each other with the fat sides facing out. Interlace the bones like fingers so that they hold still in the pan. (This way you don't need to get involved with a big roasting pan.) When the oven

is up to temperature, put the pan in the oven and roast for 15 minutes, or until the internal temperature of the meat registers 125°F. on an instant-read thermometer stuck into the center of the meat.

> Meanwhile, let the garlic and shallots cool enough until they can be handled comfortably. Squeeze the garlic out of its skin; peel the shallots and cut off the hard cores.

> When the lamb is cooked, place the racks on a plate to rest for 10 minutes. Pour the fat out of the frying pan, leaving whatever browned bits have accumulated (that means you'll need to leave a little fat in the pan because the brown bits will be suspended in there).

> Now you'll make the sauce. Use an oven mitt because the handle of the frying pan will remain very hot during this procedure. Put the pan on top of the stove and add the wine and the peeled shallots and garlic. Bring to a boil and cook until the wine is reduced by half, 3 to 4 minutes. When the lamb has rested for 10 minutes, there will be an accumulation of juices on the plate. Add that to the sauce and cook to thicken the sauce again, another minute or two. Taste for seasoning. Swirl the butter into the sauce if you'd like it a little silkier.

> To serve, put the racks on a cutting board. Cut between the bones with a large knife to divide into chops (or, if you like, you can cut double chops). Divide the meat among 4 plates, arranging the chops with the bones pointing in toward the center of each plate. Divide the roasted vegetables among the plates and spoon the sauce over the meaty part of the chops.

✳ A word about lamb

If you think you don't like lamb, or if you haven't tried it lately, give it another go. I eat as much lamb as I do beef. People who think it's strong or "gamey" are probably thinking about the mutton people used to serve in the seventies; today's grass-fed lamb from Australia, New Zealand, and Colorado is fantastic with nothing but a little garlic and rosemary—and it definitely doesn't need to be beaten into submission with a mint jelly.

8 / **Vegetables**

For cooking purposes, vegetables divide themselves obligingly into just a few categories: quick-cooking vegetables (usually, but not always, green), such as broccoli, snow peas, string beans, cauliflower, and asparagus; tender leafy greens, such as spinach and Swiss chard; root vegetables, such as turnips, carrots, and butternut squash; potatoes—which I love—a category unto themselves; and legumes, such as lentils, chick peas, and kidney beans.

The great thing about such a categorization is that once you've figured out where your vegetable falls, you can find a number of ways to cook it. Also, if there's a particular preparation that you like, you can eat several different vegetables cooked that way. So for instance: Your aunt Mabel gave you a wok for Christmas and you want to know what to do with it. Most quick-cooking vegetables can be stir-fried quite easily. Go ahead. Experiment.

If you can't think of anything else to do with them, quick-cooking vegetables can always be blanched: simmered in rapidly boiling, *salted* water (very important—the vegetable absorbs the salt as it cooks), until they're cooked the way you like them. Usually I prefer my vegetables lightly cooked and still a little crunchy, although sometimes I love green beans Southern style—that is, boiled until they've lost lots of texture and color, and flavored with salty ham or pork. When you're cooking in the more contemporary, crispy style, note that the water must be boiling when you add a green vegetable so that it stays green. Drain the vegetable, and then toss it with a little butter, olive oil, lemon juice, vinaigrette, soy sauce, sesame oil, grated zest of whatever citrus you have on hand . . . you get the picture.

Legumes have gotten kind of a bad rap—they've been associated too long with health food and uninspired vegetarian menus. Not fair. The category encompasses all those beans and lentils we don't seem to eat much of but which make wonderfully satisfying one-pot meals with or without meat.

Dried lentils cook quickly, 20 to 30 minutes. But dried beans take much longer, from 1 to 2 hours, so I sometimes use canned. They might not have the flavor of a pot of freshly cooked beans, but they have the advantage of convenience. It pays to experiment with different brands of canned beans. Some are more cooked than others (some are downright mushy), some are saltier, and some have better flavor. Rinse canned beans well in a colander before cooking.

Sautéed broccoli with garlic and parmigiano

Broccoli tastes kind of fresh and green if you barely cook it; if you cook it a little longer, it develops a deeper flavor. And if you cook it too long, it breaks down into a flavorless, colorless mash. You can go either crispy or soft with this recipe, which is essentially a method of steaming the broccoli in olive oil and garlic so that the vegetable absorbs their flavors. If you like, add a little more fresh extra-virgin olive oil for serving. This is also very good at room temperature or cold. The recipe will work equally well with string beans, asparagus, or cauliflower; if using cauliflower, you'll need to cook it for 5 to 7 minutes.

SERVES 4 / WINE PAIRING: Soave

1¼ pounds broccoli crowns (see Note)
3 tablespoons extra-virgin olive oil, plus a little extra for drizzling
2 garlic cloves, thinly sliced
¼ teaspoon crushed red pepper flakes (optional)
½ teaspoon kosher salt
Juice of ½ lemon (1 to 2 tablespoons)
2 tablespoons freshly grated Parmigiano-Reggiano

> Cut the broccoli into little florets, about 2 inches long. In a large, deep frying pan over medium-high heat, combine the oil, garlic, and red pepper flakes, if using. Cook the garlic and pepper, stirring, until the garlic sizzles, about 1 minute. Add the broccoli, sprinkle with the salt, and stir for 1 to 2 minutes. Add ½ cup water, cover, and cook for 2 to 3 minutes, until the broccoli is just barely tender. Uncover the pan, raise the heat, and cook until the water evaporates, 1 to 2 minutes longer. Spoon the broccoli into a bowl and give it a squeeze of lemon juice. Drizzle with a little olive oil, sprinkle with the Parmigiano, and serve.

NOTE: Most supermarkets sell broccoli "crowns" these days—that is, heads of broccoli from which a good piece of the stem has been lopped off, so that you get mostly tender florets, and less stem. If you can't find crowns, buy 2 pounds whole broccoli and remove the stems.

Stir-fried broccoli with garlic and soy

This is a surefire technique for almost any quick-cooking green vegetable such as snow peas, sugar snap peas, asparagus, or even Brussels sprouts (if you can, get small young ones, or cut the regular-size models in half). *Haricots verts*, those skinny, dark-green, pricey string beans from France, cook up beautifully this way. Know that any quantity over about 3/4 pound doesn't cook evenly at all in a wok.

SERVES 4 / WINE PAIRING: Demi-Sec Chenin Blanc

1 tablespoon pine nuts
3 tablespoons peanut oil
1¼ pounds broccoli crowns (see Note, opposite)
1 garlic clove, crushed
2 tablespoons soy sauce
1 teaspoon balsamic vinegar

> Toast the pine nuts in the dry wok over medium heat, shaking the pan often to keep the nuts from getting too brown, until evenly golden, 3 to 5 minutes. Remove the nuts to a small bowl.

> Heat the oil in a large wok over a high flame. When the oil is hot, add the broccoli and cook, stirring, for 3 to 5 minutes, until it is almost tender. Add the garlic and cook for 30 seconds, until you can smell garlic but it hasn't browned. Then add the soy sauce and the toasted pine nuts and stir it all together for another minute; the broccoli should be cooked by now. If not, cook for another minute. Toss with the balsamic vinegar, dump out into a bowl, and serve.

+ *VARIATION:* Sugar Snap Peas with Pine Nuts and Shiitakes
Follow the recipe above using sugar snap peas (don't forget to remove the tough strings from them first), but cook the peas for about 5 minutes total. About halfway through the cooking time, add the toasted pine nuts and ¼ pound shiitake mushroom caps that have been halved or quartered, depending on their size.

+ *VARIATION:* Brussels Sprouts with Turmeric and Lemon
This works best with tiny Brussels sprouts. Follow the recipe above using Brussels sprouts (tiny ones whole; large ones halved), but add ½ teaspoon turmeric and ½ teaspoon salt along with the sprouts. Omit the soy sauce and balsamic vinegar. Stop cooking them before they get mushy. Squeeze lemon juice over before serving.

+ *VARIATION:* Haricots Verts with Soy and Pine Nuts
Follow the recipe above, cooking the green beans for 3 to 4 minutes.

Southern-style green beans

These are not the currently fashionable, barely cooked, bright-green veggies you're seeing in trendy restaurants. These are the green beans I grew up with, the kind that my grandma Daisy cooked until they were so soft and tender you barely needed teeth to eat them—and I love them that way. Just don't cook them so long that they lose *all* color and texture; it's not as if your jaw is wired shut (one hopes). A little bacon and/or onion and/or smoky ham gives a nice kick.

SERVES 4 / WINE PAIRING: Light to Medium Crozes Hermitage

2 to 3 strips of bacon, cut into 2-inch pieces
1 medium onion, sliced
1$\frac{1}{2}$ pounds string beans, ends trimmed, cut into 2-inch lengths
$\frac{1}{2}$ teaspoon kosher salt
$\frac{1}{2}$ teaspoon freshly ground black pepper

> Combine the bacon and onion in a 2-quart saucepan and cook, stirring, over medium heat until the bacon renders its fat and the onion is translucent, about 5 minutes. Add the beans and stir. Add 1 cup water and the salt, cover, and cook until the beans are very tender, 15 to 20 minutes. Remove to a bowl with a slotted spoon and add the pepper. Serve hot.

Roasted string beans with shallots

This is another long-cooking method for beans, not for the crisp-vegetable crowd. The shallots get very sweet with roasting. Add a squeeze of lemon or a little vinegar if you like, or toss in some chopped thyme.

SERVES 4 / WINE PAIRING: Juicy, fruity Riesling or Beaujolais

1$\frac{1}{2}$ pounds string beans, ends trimmed
2 large shallots, cut into $\frac{1}{4}$-inch slices
2 tablespoons extra-virgin olive oil
$\frac{1}{2}$ teaspoon kosher salt
$\frac{1}{8}$ teaspoon freshly ground black pepper

> Preheat the oven to 400°F.

> Toss the beans and shallots with the oil and salt on a baking sheet. Roast, stirring twice during roasting, until the shallots have caramelized and the beans are beginning to brown and wilt, about 25 minutes. Sprinkle with the pepper and serve hot.

+ *VARIATION:* Roasted Asparagus
Substitute asparagus and roast for about 10 minutes.

Cauliflower purée (a.k.a. low–carb mashed "potatoes")

Cauliflower is a vegetable that, until recently, I have had little use for. I just never liked the flavor, color, or texture. And then, at the peak of the low-carb craze, my friend Regina whipped up a purée of cauliflower, which has far fewer carbohydrates than potatoes, and I was absolutely blown away. First of all, in my view mashed potatoes really serve primarily as a silky, textural vehicle for butter, cream, and salt. Cauliflower does almost as nice a job. I'm not saying I'm giving up potatoes, but this is really very good.

Steaming works better than boiling for this purée because boiling leaches flavor out of the cauliflower. You can get a big pot with a steamer insert anywhere for about twenty dollars. But go ahead and boil if you need to—just use less liquid to thin the purée. The cauliflower absorbs water in boiling.

There's no law that says you can't purée other quick-cooking vegetables as well: Imagine whirled peas, if you will—the bright green color looks fantastic on a plate.

SERVES 4 / WINE PAIRING: Medium-bodied Côtes du Rhône

1 head of cauliflower, 2 to $2^{1}/_{2}$ pounds
3 tablespoons unsalted butter
1 teaspoon kosher salt
$^{1}/_{4}$ teaspoon freshly ground black pepper

> Pull the leaves off the cauliflower and cut out the core in a kind of cone-shaped section. Then pull the florets off the head with your fingers, using a knife when you need to. Break or cut the florets into smaller, regular pieces (about $1^{1}/_{2}$ inch) and put them in the steamer insert. Bring about 1 inch of water to a boil in the steamer pot, add the insert, cover, and cook for about 15 minutes, or until you can poke a paring knife into the stems and you can feel that there's still a little texture there. Stir the cauliflower well a few times while it's steaming so that it cooks evenly.

> Dump about half of the cauliflower into a food processor. Measure out $^{3}/_{4}$ cup of the steaming liquid, and pour in about $^{1}/_{4}$ cup; purée until smooth. Now dump the rest of the cauliflower on top, add about one third of the remaining liquid, and purée again. You'll need to stop and scrape and stir the purée a few times; add more liquid as you need to, but as little as possible—you want flavor and a fluffy texture. With the motor running, process in the butter, salt, and pepper through the feed tube. Taste for seasoning and serve hot. (You can reheat over low heat in the same pan if you're not eating immediately.)

NOTE: Cauliflower is an excellent canvas for other flavors. I like things spicy and I love mustard, so I sometimes add a tablespoon of Colman's, the hot English mustard powder, to this purée. You might also add curry powder, grated Parmigiano, crumbled blue cheese, or a chopped fresh herb.

Sautéed spinach with garlic and pecorino cheese

Spinach is never better than when it's wilted in olive oil with garlic and topped with grated cheese. You can use this same technique in a couple of different ways—see the variations below for ideas.

The "correct" way to clean spinach is to strip the stem off each leaf. But I have no patience for it. I strip off just the thick (or otherwise unappetizing) stems and I'm quite happy to eat the thinner ones: They taste fine and they're probably good for you. But when you're showing off for the in-laws, maybe it's worth the hassle.

If you're a big fan of garlic, feel free to add another chopped clove with the salt at the end of cooking.

SERVES 4 / WINE PAIRING: New Zealand Sauvignon Blanc or full-bodied Trebbiano

3 tablespoons extra-virgin olive oil

2 whole garlic cloves, smashed

1 pound spinach, thick stems removed, leaves rinsed and spun dry
    in a salad spinner

1/2 teaspoon kosher salt

1/8 teaspoon freshly ground black pepper

Juice of 1 lemon (about 2 tablespoons)

1/4 cup freshly grated Pecorino Romano

> Heat the oil in a large frying pan over a medium flame. Add the garlic and cook until lightly brown, 3 to 4 minutes. Crank the heat up to medium high, add the spinach and cook, stirring, until wilted, about 2 minutes. (If your pan isn't large enough to handle all of the spinach at once, put in about half, stir until it wilts down, and then put in the rest.) Sprinkle with the salt and cook for 1 more minute. Take the pan off the heat, season with the pepper, and squeeze the lemon over. Sprinkle with the cheese and serve hot or at room temperature.

+ *VARIATION:* **Asian-Style Spinach**
Cook as in the recipe above but omit the cheese, and season with a drizzle of sesame oil and soy sauce, plus about 1 teaspoon toasted sesame seeds.

+ *VARIATION:* **Buttery Spinach**
Replace the oil with butter and omit the garlic.

+ *VARIATION.* **Creamed Spinach**
Wilt the spinach as in the recipe above and remove it from the pan. Add $1/2$ cup cream and a pinch of freshly grated nutmeg to the pan and cook until reduced and quite thick, 2 to 3 minutes. Add the spinach and at least 1 tablespoon butter (2 tablespoons is even better, if you feel like you can afford it) and toss; don't cook much longer or the spinach will start to give off water and thin the cream. Season with a squeeze of lemon, $1/2$ teaspoon salt, $1/8$ teaspoon pepper, and cheese, if you like.

+ *VARIATION:* **Sautéed Swiss Chard with Garlic and Pecorino**
Follow the recipe above, but use stemmed chard leaves.

Grilled corn with ground chilies

This is the simplest way I know to cook corn. Tastes great with anything.

SERVES 4 / WINE PAIRING: Fruity Chardonnay

6 ears of corn, shucked
Unsalted butter to taste
$3/4$ teaspoon kosher salt
$1/4$ teaspoon ground, dried chili pepper (cayenne or any other sort)

> Build a fire in a charcoal grill or preheat a gas grill (see page 85). Put the corn on the grill over medium-high heat, cover, and grill until lightly browned and softened, about 7 minutes. Turn the corn as it begins to brown and don't overcook it; bite into it if you have a question about whether it's done.

> Spread the corn with butter, sprinkle each ear with $1/8$ teaspoon salt and a pinch of chili pepper, and serve immediately.

Rosemary roasted vegetables

A simple, terrific fall or winter side dish. If your carrots and parsnips have particularly thick ends, cut these sections in half lengthwise before slicing. You want a relatively uniform thickness, for even cooking. Of course, it doesn't matter at all if you have these exact proportions of turnips to potatoes—any combo works.

SERVES 4 / WINE PAIRING: New Zealand Sauvignon Blanc or Dry Vouvray

$1/2$ pound parsnips, peeled, trimmed, and cut into $1^1/2$-inch lengths
$1/2$ pound carrots, peeled, trimmed, and cut into $1^1/2$-inch lengths
$1/2$ pound turnips, peeled, trimmed, and cut into $1/2$-inch wedges
$1/2$ pound sweet potatoes, peeled and cut into $1^1/2 \times 1/2$-inch sections
6 medium shallots, peeled
2 tablespoons extra-virgin olive oil
$3/4$ teaspoon kosher salt
2 tablespoons fresh rosemary needles
1 head of garlic, broken up into cloves (with skin)
$1/4$ teaspoon freshly ground black pepper

> Preheat the oven to 400°F.

> In a 9×13-inch baking dish, toss the parsnips, carrots, turnips, sweet potatoes, and shallots with the oil and salt. Roast for 25 minutes. Add the rosemary and garlic, toss again, and continue roasting until the vegetables are browned and tender, another 20 to 25 minutes. Scrape out into a serving dish, sprinkle with the pepper, and serve hot.

Roasted potatoes with garlic and herbs

Another incredibly simple way to revel in the glorious spud. You can make this recipe with red-skinned or those long, skinny fingerlings, too. Their texture will be finer and creamier than baking potatoes. Here's one of my favorite moments in the kitchen: After you've tossed the potatoes, oil, and herbs, put your nose in the bowl and smell deeply . . . mmm. Heaven.

SERVES 4 / WINE PAIRING: Ripe Gruner Veltliner

2 pounds baking potatoes, peeled and cut into 1 1/4- to 1 1/2-inch cubes
3 tablespoons extra-virgin olive oil
3/4 teaspoon kosher salt
1 tablespoon whole plus 2 teaspoons chopped mixed fresh herbs, such as
      marjoram, oregano, and thyme
1 medium head of garlic, broken into cloves and peeled
1/4 teaspoon freshly ground black pepper

> Preheat the oven to 400°F.

> Toss the potatoes with 2 tablespoons of the oil, the salt, and the 1 tablespoon of whole mixed herbs in a 9 × 13-inch baking dish or a small roasting pan. Roast, flipping every 15 minutes with a spatula for even browning, until browned and tender, 45 to 50 minutes. About 30 minutes into the cooking, add the garlic and stir to coat with the oil.

> Remove from the oven and scrape out into a serving bowl. Add the pepper, chopped herbs, and the remaining tablespoon of olive oil. Toss and serve immediately.

✷ Potatoes

Personally, I can't live without potatoes, and I love them in almost any preparation: boiled, sautéed, oven-roasted, smashed—and they're particularly lovely in a creamy, cheesy gratin. Check out some of the different varieties available: Yukon Golds, blue Peruvians, fingerlings, Russian "bananas." Reds and russetts are just the beginning.

My favorite potato gratin

This is a cheesy, gooey gratin that tastes more of cheese than of cream, and also very subtly of fresh thyme and garlic. If you want something really simple, forget the thyme and garlic. If you want to try something different, add a layer of prosciutto or roasted red pepper strips in the center, substitute ½ pound of turnips for some potatoes, use half blue cheese, or add a layer of sliced tomatoes.

SERVES 4 TO 6 / WINE PAIRING: Trebbiano or Light Rosé

1 tablespoon unsalted butter, plus more for greasing pan
2 pounds baking potatoes
½ teaspoon kosher salt
½ teaspoon freshly ground pepper, preferably white
2 pinches freshly grated nutmeg
1 garlic clove, sliced
2 bay leaves
A couple sprigs of fresh thyme (optional)
2 firmly packed cups grated Gruyère cheese
1 cup heavy cream

> Preheat the oven to 350°F.

> Butter the inside of an 8 × 8-inch baking dish. Peel the potatoes and put them in a bowl of cold water to keep them from browning while you slice them. Slice about half of the potatoes as thin as you can and layer them into the pan. (A food processor or Benriner slicer comes in handy for this.) Sprinkle with ¼ teaspoon of the salt, ¼ teaspoon of the pepper, a pinch of nutmeg, the garlic, and the bay leaves. Strip the thyme leaves off the sprigs and sprinkle them over the potatoes. Sprinkle with half of the cheese and pour over half of the cream.

> Now slice and layer the remaining potatoes on top and sprinkle again with ¼ teaspoon salt, ¼ teaspoon pepper, and a pinch of nutmeg. Pour the rest of the cream over, sprinkle with the rest of the cheese, and dot with the 1 tablespoon butter (a great trick: use a frozen stick of butter and a grater). Put the gratin in the oven and bake until the top is golden and crusty and the interior of the gratin is still moist with cream when you stick a knife into it, about 1 hour and 15 minutes. Let it sit for 10 minutes before serving to let it firm up; it will be much easier to cut and serve.

+ *VARIATION:* **Butternut Squash Gratin with Parmigiano**
Using a 2 ¼- to 2 ½-pound butternut squash, trim off both ends. Cut the squash in half where the neck joins the rounded body. Cut both halves in half again lengthwise. Working with the neck end, peel both halves with a vegetable peeler (or stand the halves on end and cut off the skin with a large knife). Cut both halves crosswise into thin slices. Now scoop out the seeds from the rounded end. Peel with a vegetable peeler or cut into sections that you can peel easily with the knife; halve (if you haven't already cut into pieces) and thinly slice.

Assemble the gratin just as for the potato gratin, but use 1 cup Gruyère cheese (about 4 ounces) and $^1/_2$ cup Parmigiano-Reggiano (about 1 ounce), and $^3/_4$ cup cream. Add 10 basil leaves, torn into pieces, along with the garlic and bay leaves. Bake for 1 hour, or until the top is golden and crusty.

Mashed potatoes

Not all potatoes are alike—not at all. Mashed potatoes are traditionally made with baking potatoes to produce a fluffy texture. But you can use Yukon Golds or new potatoes, too—they'll just give you a smoother, tighter texture. The big deal is not to get overzealous and stir them too much; the more you mix, the more you develop the potato starch (particularly in baking potatoes) so that quite quickly you'll end up with a gluey mess.

I've given a range for butter and cream because the truth is, as far as I'm concerned, the more you put in the better it tastes; but some people find a whole stick of butter a little scary. So start with the lower end and add what you like. You can also thin the potatoes with more half-and-half, cream, or milk—even skim milk, if that's how you feel. For a change, stir a big spoonful of pesto into the potatoes at the end, or use some Porcini Butter (page 137) in place of plain butter.

SERVES 4 TO 6

2 pounds baking potatoes, peeled
Kosher salt for boiling, plus more to taste
$^3/_4$ cup half-and-half, cream, or whole milk
4 to 8 tablespoons unsalted butter (see head note)
$^1/_4$ teaspoon freshly ground black pepper

> Cut the potatoes into pieces (cut them big or little, it doesn't matter what size, but keep them uniform—the larger the pieces, the longer the cooking time) and put them in a medium saucepan. Add cold water to cover and then enough salt so that the water tastes salty (1 teaspoon per quart of water). Bring the water to a boil, reduce the heat to low, and simmer until the potatoes are tender, 10 to 15 minutes. Drain in a colander.

> In a large saucepan, combine the half-and-half and butter and warm over medium heat to melt the butter. Add the drained potatoes and mash with a potato masher; then stir it all up together. Season with salt and stir in the pepper.

+ *VARIATION:* Mashed Turnips
Replace the potatoes with turnips.

+ *VARIATION:* Mashed Potatoes and Celeriac
Replace 1 pound of the potatoes with $1^1/_4$ pound celeriac (cut off all of the brown skin and any knobby stuff), and continue with the recipe.

Black beans with linguiça sausage and chipotle chili

Vegetables, a chipotle chili, and linguiça—a type of Portuguese sausage—give black beans a rich, smoky, mildly spicy taste. If you have a food processor, use it to chop the vegetables; you're going to use it to purée the chili with the beans anyway and, unless you're really quick with the knife, it will cut your work time significantly. One chili will give a mild heat; add another half if you like your beans distinctly spicy. This recipe works nicely with kidney beans as well. If you can't find linguiça, substitute andouille, chorizo, or even spicy Italian sausage, or omit the sausage entirely. Serve over rice.

SERVES 4 / WINE PAIRING: Full-bodied Spanish Ribera del Duero

6 medium garlic cloves

1 medium onion, quartered

1 red bell pepper, stemmed, seeded, and quartered

2 tablespoons extra-virgin olive oil

$1/2$ pound linguiça sausage (see head note), cut on the diagonal $1/4$ inch thick

$1^{1}/2$ teaspoons whole cumin seeds

2 bay leaves

$1^{1}/2$ teaspoons dried oregano or 1 tablespoon fresh

$1/4$ teaspoon kosher salt

6 cups cooked black beans (2 29-ounce cans), drained and rinsed

$1^{1}/2$ cups canned low-sodium chicken stock

1 canned chipotle chili in adobo

1 tablespoon fresh lime juice (from about 1 lime)

$1/2$ cup chopped fresh cilantro (leaves and tender stems)

> If using a food processor, put the garlic in the processor and process to coarsely chop. (It won't get chopped fine enough if you chop it with the other vegetables.) Then add the onion and bell pepper and process to coarsely chop everything. Or, if working with a knife, mince the garlic and chop the onion and bell pepper.

> Heat the oil in a large saucepan over a medium flame. Add the sausage and cook to brown lightly and render the fat, 4 to 5 minutes. With a slotted spoon, remove the sausage to a plate, and set aside. Add the cumin to the pan and stir until fragrant, about 60 seconds. Add the chopped vegetables, bay leaves, oregano, and salt. Cook, stirring every now and then, until the vegetables are tender, about 10 minutes. (The vegetables will give off a lot of liquid; when it evaporates, they will be done.) Add the beans and stock. Bring to a boil, reduce the heat, and simmer for 5 minutes.

> Scoop out about 1 cup beans with liquid and purée in the food processor with the chipotle chili. Return the purée to the saucepan along with the reserved linguiça and continue cooking for 5 more minutes to blend the flavors. Remove the bay leaves. Stir in the lime juice and cilantro and serve over rice.

Lentils braised in stock

Lentils are great at room temperature (or at least given a few minutes to cool), when you can really taste their flavor. And an extra tablespoon of olive oil drizzled over the lentils before serving won't hurt either.

I like the lentils with the hulls because they don't get mushy. Varieties include *lentilles de Puy* (French lentils), beluga lentils, or, at Indian grocers a type of brown lentil sold as *masoor dal*. The lentils in the supermarket have been hulled; they're also fine to use, they'll just make more of a soupy texture. But they also cook more quickly. Count on 30 minutes for lentils with hulls and 20 minutes for the supermarket variety.

SERVES 4 / WINE PAIRING: Light-bodied Cabernet Franc

3 tablespoons extra-virgin olive oil
1 medium onion, chopped
1 medium carrot, chopped
1 celery stalk (from the heart), chopped
3 garlic cloves, minced
1 bay leaf
1/2 teaspoon dried thyme
1/4 teaspoon kosher salt, plus more to taste
1 pound lentils (about 2 1/2 cups), preferably with the hull
6 cups canned low-sodium chicken stock
1/4 teaspoon freshly ground black pepper

> In a medium saucepan, heat 2 tablespoons of the oil over a medium flame. Add the onion, carrot, celery, garlic, bay leaf, thyme, and salt. Cook for 3 to 4 minutes, until the vegetables are wilted. Add the lentils and stock and bring to a boil. Reduce the heat so that the lentils just simmer, place the lid to partially cover, and cook until the lentils are tender, about 20 minutes for hulled lentils, 30 minutes for lentils with the hull. Stir in the remaining tablespoon of olive oil, the pepper, and additional salt, if you need it, depending on the saltiness of the stock.

+ *VARIATION:* Lentils with Portobello Mushrooms, Garlic, and Parsley
Stem and cut 2 large portobello mushrooms in half, then slice crosswise. Heat 1 tablespoon olive oil in the saucepan. Add the mushrooms and cook, stirring, until tender, 2 to 3 minutes. Remove from the heat and stir in 1 small garlic clove, minced, and 2 tablespoons chopped flat-leaf parsley. Scrape that out into a bowl. Make the recipe as above and add the mushroom mixture at the end of cooking; cook for 1 minute to warm them up.

+ *VARIATION:* **Lentils with Bacon and Sherry Vinegar**
Cook ½ pound thick-cut slab bacon, sliced crosswise ¼ inch thick, in the saucepan over medium heat with no added oil, to render the fat, about 5 minutes. Remove the bacon from the pan, leaving the rendered fat. Now add the vegetables and herbs (omit the olive oil) and continue cooking as in the recipe above. When cooked, stir in the reserved bacon and 1 tablespoon sherry vinegar and simmer for 1 minute to blend the flavors.

+ *VARIATION:* **Lentils with Indian Spices**
Cook the lentils as in the recipe above. But before adding the herbs, cook 1½ teaspoons cumin in the oil for 30 to 60 seconds, until you can smell it. Then add ½ teaspoon turmeric with the stock and lentils. And stir in ¼ cup chopped cilantro at the end of cooking. (This is really a type of Indian *dal*—dishes of cooked legumes, often but by no means always lentils—that are served at various degrees of thickness depending on personal preference. If you'd like a thicker mixture, remove about 1 cup lentils and cooking liquid at the end of cooking, mash to a purée, and return to the pot.

✳ Cooking dried beans

If you have a couple of hours to spare and want to cook dried beans, here's how. Some folks soak beans before cooking. I don't. Soaking doesn't decrease the cooking time enormously, and it requires planning ahead. This basic recipe will work for any kind of dried bean such as kidney beans, black beans, chickpeas, cannellini, and Great Northern beans. The wide range of cooking time is due to the fact that like everything else, beans get old, and the older they are, the longer they take to cook.

So: Eyeball the beans and pick through them to remove any small stones or other debris. Then put the beans in a large pot with cold water to cover generously (3 quarts water to 1 pound dried beans is a standard ratio). For 1 pound dried beans, add 1 chopped onion, 1 small head of garlic peeled and cut in half, 2 bay leaves, and 1 table-spoon kosher salt. A ham hock gives beans great flavor if you're cooking for a meat-eating crowd. Bring to a boil and use a spoon to skim off the gray foam. Cook the beans at a gentle simmer, partially covered, for 1 to 2 hours, until they are very tender. If the water level drops, add more; the beans should always be covered with water. Pick out the garlic and bay leaves. Cut the meat off the ham hock, shred it, and mix it into the beans.

Vegetarians, ho:
roasted butternut squash pie

You've planned a dinner at home for a new love interest. The date is set, you're already relishing the menu you've devised, and you give a call just to check whether the candidate is violently allergic to anything you're planning to cook. And then you find out that not only do you have a vegetarian on your hands, but a *vegan*—someone who not only doesn't eat meat, but also eats no dairy, eggs, or fish. What do you do? Cook this! The crazy thing is, it's really, *really* delicious. I make it all the time, even when no vegans are coming over.

Serve this with a salad, and it's dinner. You can assemble it ahead and refrigerate, then bake.

SERVES 4 TO 6 / WINE PAIRING: Ripe Gewürtztraminer or rich, fruity Pinot Noir

$1/2$ package (1 pound) frozen filo dough

1 butternut squash (about $2^{1}/2$ pounds)

2 medium red onions, sliced through the equator $1/2$ inch thick

1 red bell pepper, halved, stemmed, and seeded

2 teaspoons kosher salt

5 tablespoons extra-virgin olive oil, plus $1/3$ cup for brushing the filo,
   or as needed

1 tablespoon finely chopped ginger (about 1 inch, peeled)

1 teaspoon ground cumin

$1/4$ teaspoon ground cinnamon

$1/4$ cup coarsely chopped fresh cilantro

$1/4$ teaspoon freshly ground black pepper

$1/3$ cup raisins

$1/4$ cup walnut pieces

2 medium garlic cloves, chopped

1 16-ounce bag of spinach, large stems removed

$1^{1}/2$ cups Basic Tomato Sauce (page 66) or store-bought sauce

> Preheat the oven to 425°F. Remove the filo from the freezer and thaw at room temperature for 1 hour.

> Meanwhile, trim off both ends of the squash. Cut it in half crosswise where the neck joins the rounded body. Working with the neck end, peel off the tough skin with a vegetable peeler (or stand it on end and cut off the skin with a large knife). Cut into 3-inch chunks. Cut the rounded end in half and scoop out and discard the seeds. Peel with a vegetable peeler or a knife and cut into 3-inch chunks.

> Put the squash chunks, onions slices, and red pepper halves on a baking sheet so that the vegetables are in a single layer. Sprinkle with 1 teaspoon of the salt and 3 tablespoons of the oil. Toss to coat the vegetables with the oil. Roast for 30

RECIPE CONTINUES

minutes, turning the vegetables once with a spatula. Remove the pepper halves and turn everything again. Roast for 10 more minutes, or until the vegetables are tender and lightly browned. Dump the squash into a large bowl. Quarter the onion slices and cut the pepper into 1-inch cubes; dump them both into the bowl. Sprinkle the vegetables with the ginger, cumin, cinnamon, cilantro, 1/2 teaspoon salt, and the pepper. Add the raisins and toss gently; set aside.

> Turn the oven temperature down to 375°F. Put the walnuts on a baking sheet and toast in the oven, shaking the pan twice for even cooking, until lightly browned, 5 to 7 minutes. Remove from the oven and chop; dump them into the bowl with the vegetables and stir gently.

> Meanwhile, heat the remaining 2 tablespoons olive oil with the garlic in a large frying pan over a medium flame. Cook, stirring occasionally, for 2 minutes to flavor the oil. Add about one third of the spinach and cook, turning it in the oil with tongs, until wilted, about 1 minute. Add more spinach and cook, turning as before, and then add the remaining spinach. Sprinkle with the remaining 1/2 teaspoon salt and cook until all the spinach is wilted, 2 to 3 minutes total.

> To assemble the pie, have ready a 9 × 13-inch baking dish and a pastry brush. Pour 1/3 cup olive oil into a small bowl. Set that on a work area with the filo and the vegetables. Open the package of thawed filo and unroll the pastry sheets so that they lie flat. Brush the baking dish with olive oil. Arrange the dish so that one long side faces you. Starting at the left edge of the dish, lay one sheet of filo in the dish crosswise so that it covers about half of the bottom, and half of the sheet hangs over the side facing you. Brush the part that covers the bottom with olive oil. Now lay a second sheet along the right-hand side of the dish, overlapping the first sheet in the middle of the dish and overhanging the side facing you. Brush with olive oil. Repeat with 2 more sheets but this time arrange them in the dish so that they overhang the other long side of the dish (at the top). Continue in the same way until you've used 14 sheets of filo. (As you're working, you'll come across some sheets of pastry that stick together and rip. Discard them if you need to—you have more sheets than you need.)

> Line the bottom of the dish with about half of the spinach, using your hands to open up the leaves and spread them out. Spoon the squash mixture on top and gently flatten with the spoon. Cover with the rest of the spinach. Working with the side of the dish facing you, fold one of the filo sheets over the filling and brush with oil. Fold the sheet next to it over and brush with oil. Do the same for 2 sheets on the opposing side of the dish. Continue in this way until all of the filo is folded over the filling. Then cover with 2 more sheets of filo, brushing each with more oil. (You may run out of oil. That's fine, just pour more into the dish.)

> Put the baking dish in the oven and bake until the pastry is golden brown, 30 to 35 minutes. Let stand for 15 minutes before serving, or let cool to room temperature. Warm the tomato sauce over medium heat. Cut the pie into squares and serve with the tomato sauce.

White beans with tomato, oregano, and feta cheese

These beans make a great vegetarian meal or an accompaniment to lamb. Use firm canned cannellini beans such as Progresso. This recipe works fine with chickpeas, too.

SERVES 4 AS A MAIN COURSE, 6 AS A SIDE / WINE PAIRING: Trebbiano or Crisp Greek Mantinia

3 tablespoons extra-virgin olive oil, plus extra for drizzling

1 medium onion, chopped

2 teaspoons chopped fresh oregano

2 bay leaves

$1/2$ teaspoon kosher salt

1 pound plum tomatoes, halved

6 cups cooked cannellini beans (three 19-ounce cans), drained and rinsed

$3/4$ cup canned low-sodium chicken stock

$1 1/4$ cups crumbled sheep's-milk (or combination sheep's- and goat's-milk) feta cheese (see Note)

2 tablespoons chopped flat-leaf parsley

$1/4$ teaspoon freshly ground black pepper

> Heat 3 tablespoons of the oil in a large, deep skillet over a medium flame. Add the onion, oregano, bay leaves, and salt and cook until the onion is wilted and tender, 5 to 7 minutes. Meanwhile, turn the tomato halves cut sides down and squeeze out the seeds over the sink. Put a grater in a large bowl. Holding the tomato halves skin side out, grate them on the large holes of a grater; throw away the skins.

> When the onion is cooked, add the tomatoes, beans, and stock to the pan and bring to a simmer. Simmer for 5 minutes, stirring every now and then, to marry the flavors. Using a rubber scraper, scrape the stew out into a bowl and let it cool for about 5 minutes. (Otherwise the feta will melt into it.) Remove the bay leaves. Gently stir in the cheese, parsley, and pepper. Drizzle with olive oil (start with 1 tablespoon) and serve hot or at room temperature.

NOTE: If you can, buy imported feta (Greek or French) made from sheep's milk, or a combination of goat's and sheep's milk. The supermarket may carry a rather plastic-textured, commercial cow's-milk feta; the taste and texture are far inferior.

9 / **Desserts and breakfast**

In Paris, one of the top food capitals on the planet, nobody makes dessert at home. They make elaborate multicourse dinners and pair everything expertly with the perfect wines, but they don't bother with baking. Neither would you if you could step out your door and choose among the incredible array of beautiful pastry shops that Paris has on every block, each of them producing more fantastic, jewel-like creations than the last. But since you probably don't live in Paris (at least not year round) the fantasia of pies, cakes, and croissants offered by your grocery-store bakery might be somewhat less alluring. So you have to make dessert.

You don't need to spend months learning how to make some brilliant pastry. But just as you need to have something for people to eat and drink when they walk in your door, so must you send them off with a sweet. It leaves your guests feeling satiated and well taken care of. It needn't be fancy or labor intensive. Some ripe fruit and an excellent cheese or two are as lovely a way to end a meal as I know (and it gives you something to eat while you polish off the leftover wine). Here is a collection of dead-simple dessert recipes (and don't forget about Warm Caramel Brownie Sundaes, back up front on page 20—because ice cream is probably what *everybody* really wants).

Beyond dessert, is it now morning and your dinner date is still in your apartment? Congratulations! So you need to take care of breakfast. Outsource the breads and coffee cakes—chances are, you don't want to be mucking around for too long in the kitchen when you could be getting back to bed . . .

There are a few quick breakfast things you should know how to make, chief among them, coffee (but I'm gonna trust you already have that one handled). You probably have all the ingredients in your refrigerator anyway. All of the dishes here can be served for brunch or a casual dinner as well.

Chocolate-glazed almond butter cake

This buttery cake gets its tremendous punch of flavor from ground almonds and almond extract. A chocolate glaze is particularly easy to make in a microwave. The idea is to get the mixture just warm enough that it pours smoothly and adheres to the cake in a thin layer. If you don't have a microwave, use a double boiler. Or, for simplicity's sake, you can dispense with the glaze altogether and serve the cake warm as is, or sift about 2 tablespoons confectioners' sugar through a fine sieve over the top of the cooled cake.

SERVES 8

for the almond butter cake

6 ounces (1½ sticks) unsalted butter, at room temperature, plus more for greasing pan
½ cup whole blanched almonds
¾ cup granulated sugar
3 large eggs
½ teaspoon almond extract
1½ cups all-purpose flour
1 teaspoon baking powder
¼ teaspoon fine salt
½ cup buttermilk
½ teaspoon pure vanilla extract

for the dark chocolate glaze

6 ounces bittersweet or semisweet chocolate, broken into small pieces
6 tablespoons (¾ stick) unsalted butter, cut into pieces
1 teaspoon pure vanilla extract

> For the cake, preheat the oven to 350°F. and set a rack in the middle of the oven. Butter a 9-inch cake pan.

> Combine the almonds and the sugar in the bowl of a food processor and process until the almonds are finely ground. Add the 6 ounces butter and process until smooth. Scrape down the bowl and process again. Add the eggs and almond extract and process until smooth.

> In a small bowl, stir together the flour, baking powder, and salt. Add half of the dry ingredients to the batter and process until well mixed. Add half of the buttermilk and process until smooth. Add the rest of the dry ingredients and process until smooth, and then add the vanilla and the rest of the buttermilk—again, process until smooth.

> Scrape the batter out into the prepared cake pan and gently spread with a rubber spatula so that it is even. Put the pan in the oven and bake until a tester stuck in the center of the cake comes out clean, about 35 minutes. Put the pan on a rack and let

cool for 10 minutes. Turn the cake out onto the rack. You can either cut the cake into wedges and serve immediately or let it cool completely and glaze.

> For the glaze, combine the chocolate and $\frac{1}{4}$ cup water in a small microwaveable bowl or the top of a double boiler. Cover with plastic wrap and microwave on medium until just melted, 1 to $1\frac{1}{2}$ minutes; or heat over (not in) simmering water in a double boiler until melted, 1 to 2 minutes. Remove from the heat and stir in the butter, a couple of pieces at a time, until the mixture is smooth. Stir in the vanilla extract. If the chocolate cools too quickly and the butter won't melt, return the bowl to the microwave or the simmering water and rewarm for 20 seconds.

> The glaze is the right temperature when it is warm to the touch (90°F.) and the consistency of honey. Raise the spoonful of chocolate over the bowl and let the chocolate drip back in. It should mound and then slowly melt back into the chocolate. If it melts immediately, it is too hot and won't adhere to the cake; let it cool a little.

> Now place the cake on a rack over a baking sheet, domed side up. Pour the glaze all over the top of the cake—you want it to cover the top and pour down over the sides. Use a metal spatula to smooth the top and the sides, adding more glaze as needed.

New age floats

Root beer floats are a classic, which means I'm obliged to mess with them a little. These "new age" floats are made with a couple of my favorite sodas, other than root beer of course. Serve all three to each guest in fun, kitschy glasses, and see how happy people get.

The technique is the same for all of these: Pour the soda into a large glass. Add one big round scoop of ice cream and a straw, and serve immediately.

EACH RECIPE SERVES 4

black cherry floats

4 12-ounce cans black cherry soda
1 pint vanilla ice cream

creamsicle floats

4 12-ounce bottles Orangina or other orange soda
1 pint vanilla ice cream

caribbean ginger beer floats

4 12-ounce bottles Caribbean ginger beer
1 pint vanilla ice cream

Warm spiced apple tart

Puff pastry is incredibly labor-intensive and requires great skill. And a lot of time. That's why I love frozen, store-bought puff pastry. If you want flaky, beautiful pies and other fancy-looking desserts, you don't have to go to pastry school. The premade stuff tastes like puff pastry ought to, and it will allow you to make all manner of elegant desserts in very short order. To make the tart ahead, roll and cut the pastry and have it sitting in the refrigerator for up to several hours. Peel and slice the apples, arrange them cored sides down, and squeeze lemon juice over to keep them from turning brown; cover with plastic wrap and refrigerate for up to 2 hours. At the end of dinner, arrange the apple slices on the dough and stick the tart in the oven—15 minutes later you'll have dessert.

SERVES 4

1 package (1.1 pound) frozen puff pastry
3 tablespoons unsalted butter, plus more for buttering sheet
All-purpose flour, for rolling
3 Golden Delicious apples
$1/3$ cup sugar
$1/4$ teaspoon ground cinnamon
$1/2$ teaspoon ground coriander
1 large egg
$1/2$ pint whipping cream, for serving

> Thaw one sheet of puff pastry overnight in the refrigerator or just leave it out at room temperature for at least 30 minutes. It might take longer, depending on how warm it is in your kitchen. If you have any doubts, thaw it ahead of time and put it back in the refrigerator until you're ready to roll it; from the refrigerator, you'll need 10 to 15 minutes at room temperature.

> Preheat the oven to 475°F. and butter a baking sheet.

> On a lightly floured work surface, roll out the pastry sheet to a bit more than a 12-inch square. Using a plate as a guide, cut a 12-inch round. (If you have a 12-inch plate, cool. If not, use a smaller plate and cut around it with a margin of however much you need to make up the difference.) Gently pick up the pastry round with both hands and put it on the buttered baking sheet. Put this in the refrigerator while you work on the apples.

> Peel the apples. Cut them in half through the stem ends and use a melon baller or spoon to scoop out the cores. Then put the apple halves flat side down on a cutting board and trim both ends straight across. Cut the apple halves crosswise into very thin slices.

> Take the baking sheet out of the refrigerator. Arrange the apples on the pastry round in concentric circles so that the rounded sides of the slices face out, and the apple slices overlap by about $1/2$ inch. Leave a $1/2$-inch border at the edge of the tart

and arrange the apples so that the entire pastry round (with the exception of the border) is covered by the apples.

> In a small bowl, stir together the sugar, cinnamon, and coriander. Sprinkle over the apples only; any sugar on the pastry border will burn. Cut the 3 tablespoons of butter into about 20 thin slices and lay them over the apples, too. Whisk the egg in a small bowl for a glaze. Then use a pastry brush to paint the pastry border with the glaze.

> Stick the tart in the oven and bake until the apples are tender and the border is browned, 13 to 15 minutes.

> Meanwhile, whip the cream in a bowl with an electric mixer, or a whisk, until soft peaks form when you lift the beater or whisk. The cream should not be too stiff.

> When the tart is cooked, cut it immediately into quarters. Use a spatula to put one quarter on each of 4 plates and serve with the whipped cream.

Chocolate truffles

A plateful of truffles accompanied by coffee will wow your guests—the truffles literally melt in your mouth. These are astonishingly easy to make, once you get the hang of rolling the chocolates quickly—very quickly—before they melt in your hands.

Most supermarkets carry both bittersweet and semisweet chocolate as well as unsweetened; semisweet is the sweetest. Either semisweet or bittersweet will taste great in this recipe. Unsweetened chocolate will not.

MAKES 28 TRUFFLES

8 ounces bittersweet or semisweet chocolate
$1/2$ cup heavy cream
1 teaspoon pure vanilla extract
2 tablespoons brandy (optional)
$1/2$ cup cocoa powder

> Chop the chocolate into small pieces (or grate it on the large holes of a grater) and put it in a heat-proof bowl. In a very small saucepan, bring the cream just to a simmer, then pour it over the chocolate in the bowl. Let stand for about 10 minutes, or until the chocolate has melted. Stir until smooth. Or, if using a microwave, combine the chocolate and cream in the bowl, cover with microwaveable plastic wrap, and microwave on medium for 1 to $1^{1/2}$ minutes to melt the chocolate. Stir until smooth without waiting.

> Cover the mixture and let cool to room temperature for 45 minutes.

> Stir in the vanilla and the brandy, if using. Now beat with an electric mixer until the mixture is thick and light colored and holds a stiff peak when you lift the beaters from the bowl, about 1 minute. Do not overbeat. Chill in the refrigerator just until the mixture is stiff enough to hold its shape, 15 to 20 minutes.

> Sift the cocoa powder over a baking sheet. To shape the truffles, use 2 spoons to measure out walnut-size lumps of chocolate just as you would drop cookies, and drop them on the cocoa-lined baking sheet, 1 to 2 inches apart. Rub your hands in a little of the cocoa powder to keep the chocolate from sticking. Then pick up one of the lumps of chocolate and lightly roll it between the palms of your hands to form a ball. Put the truffle back on the baking sheet and roll it in the cocoa powder until it's entirely covered. Do the same with the rest of the truffles. Put all of the truffles on a plate and cover loosely with plastic wrap. Refrigerate until you're ready to serve. (They will keep refrigerated for several days.)

+ *VARIATION:* **Pistachio Truffles**
Finely chop ¾ cup shelled pistachios. Spread the pistachios out on the baking sheet in lieu of the cocoa. Spoon the truffles out onto the sheet as in the recipe above. Using a little cocoa to coat your hands (don't use too much or the nuts won't stick), roll the chocolate mixture into balls. Then roll in the pistachios, pressing the nuts gently into the chocolate.

+ *VARIATION:* **Coffee Truffles**
Omit the vanilla and replace the brandy with 2 tablespoons finely ground espresso or other strong coffee beans.

+ *VARIATION:* **Chocolate-glazed Truffles**
Make the truffles and roll them in the cocoa powder as in the recipe above. Prepare the Dark Chocolate Glaze (page 000) and pour it into a small, deep bowl or a large measuring cup. Set a wire rack on top of a baking sheet. Drop the truffles into the glaze and gently submerge them with a fork. Lift them out with a fork, let the excess drip off, and set them on the rack. Refrigerate until set. If the chocolate cools and thickens while you're working, stick it back in the microwave or over a double boiler for a few seconds to warm and melt it.

Crème brûlée

How often have we all asked ourselves this question: How can I involve a blowtorch in more of my cooking? Well, here's your answer.

This crazy-rich custard with the burnt-sugar top became popular in the eighties, and it's probably second only to chocolate cake as America's favorite decadent dessert. The original vanilla *crème brûlée,* which is French for "burnt cream," is just delicious. Use a real vanilla bean for the intoxicating flavor and aroma. With fresh raspberries, it tastes even more incredible. It is also pretty easy. The only tricky part is getting that caramel crust on the top. Some tips: Brown sugar melts more rapidly and evenly than white. Most important: A propane torch works beautifully for caramelizing—restaurants use them. You'll be using the broiler, though, unless you get hooked like I did—in which case, you can buy your own kitchen-size torch at any cooking-equipment shop, like Williams-Sonoma or Sur la Table. The broiler will give results that are slightly less even, but it's going to taste good anyway.

Crème brûlée is served chilled, so it demands a tiny bit of planning ahead. Bake it that morning for the evening, or the night before so it has several hours to chill before showtime. Traditionally it is served in individual porcelain cups, widely sold in shallow 5-inch molds or deeper 3½-inch ramekins.

SERVES 4

2 cups whipping cream
1 vanilla bean (see Note, page 185) or ½ teaspoon vanilla extract
5 large eggs
7 tablespoons granulated sugar
Pinch of fine kosher salt
¼ to ½ cup light brown sugar, depending on the size of your ramekins

> Pour the cream into a saucepan and bring just to a simmer over medium heat. Take the cream off the heat. If you're using a vanilla bean, slit it down the center lengthwise with a small knife. Pry open the 2 halves with the point of the knife and lay the halves, cut side up, on a cutting board. Use the knife to scrape out the tiny, sticky black seeds, and add them to the pot with the cream. Put the pod in, too. Cover and let steep for 10 minutes to flavor the cream. If using vanilla extract, just bring the cream to a simmer and set the cream aside.

> Bring a teapot of water to a boil. Preheat the oven to 300°F. If you're using larger ramekins, you'll need 2 racks; 1 rack for smaller ramekins.

> Meanwhile, separate the egg yolks from the whites (see "Separating Yolks from Whites," page 185). You want only the yolks for this custard. (Save the whites, if you like, to add to scrambled eggs, or if you're planning on making meringues any time soon.) Keep going until you have collected all 5 yolks in the bowl.

> Add the sugar and salt to the yolks and whisk for about 30 seconds, until the mixture turns a light yellow color and becomes thick. If you've used a vanilla bean, take it out of the pot and discard it. Whisking the egg mixture constantly, gradually pour in about one quarter of the hot cream in a thin stream. Then pour in the rest of the cream. Whisk in the vanilla extract now if that's what you're using.

> Set 4 ramekins in a baking dish. Divide the crème mixture among the ramekins. Open the oven door and pull a rack out about halfway. Put the baking dish on the rack and pour boiling water into the dish so that it comes about halfway up the ramekins. (This water bath is mandatory: The idea is that the water remains a constant temperature, too low to scramble the eggs. That way you don't end up with a frittata.) Push the rack back into the oven. Repeat with a second rack if you are using 2 baking dishes. Close the oven door. Set the timer for 30 minutes if using the 5-inch shallow molds, 40 minutes for the deeper 3½-inch ramekins.

> When the timer rings, gently pull out the oven rack and watch how the custard looks as it moves. It should have begun to set up but still shake like Jell-O. Stick a thin knife into the center of one of the custards. The center will still be wet (the knife will not be clean when you pull it out) but the mixture should be hot when you taste it. If it's not hot, put the custard back in the oven for 5 minutes. If you're not sure, take it out.

> Now carefully remove the baking dish(es) from the oven—and watch it, because that hot water could slosh onto you (or, worse, into the dessert). Ladle as much of the hot water out as you can, then gently remove all 4 ramekins from the water bath. Let cool for about 20 minutes. Then cover with plastic wrap and refrigerate until completely cold, at least 2 hours or overnight.

RECIPE CONTINUES

> When you're ready to serve, move one of the oven racks to the top position and heat the broiler to high (unless you've bought a blowtorch, in which case skip the oven instructions). Unwrap the custards and put them on a baking sheet. Sprinkle the top of each as evenly as you can with about 1 tablespoon brown sugar for the smaller ramekins, 2 tablespoons for the larger. (If the sugar is hard or has developed lumps, press it through a fine sieve with the back of a spoon.)

> If you have a blowtorch, fire it up and point it downward directly onto the sugar, moving it in a circular motion around each crème brûlée to burn the sugar to a nice dark brown. If you're using the oven, put the baking sheet under the broiler and broil until the sugar melts and caramelizes. How long this takes will depend on your broiler and how close the custard is to the heat, but start checking at 30 seconds. If one side caramelizes more quickly than the other, turn the custards for more even browning. When you can smell the caramel and see that it has melted and hardened, take the custards out. Let the custards sit at room temperature for a few minutes to cool and harden, and so your guests don't burn the roofs of their mouths. Serve immediately.

+ *VARIATION:* **Crème Brûlée with Raspberries**
Prepare the custard mixture as above, but before you pour it into the ramekins, line the bottoms of the ramekins with fresh raspberries. Pour in the custard. Bake, chill, and caramelize as in the recipe above.

NOTE: Vanilla beans, long, skinny black pods that contain sticky black seeds, give crème brûlée a particularly wonderful taste and fragrance.

✳ Separating yolks from whites

Sometimes, a recipe calls for just egg whites, or just egg yolks, meaning that you have to separate the two. You can buy an egg separator, but chefs like to use the halves of a cracked eggshell itself.

Have your work bowl nearby. Then choose a small bowl with a thin, hard edge (hard plastic works well, or Pyrex) that will break the shell cleanly. Now crack one egg on the edge of the small bowl and, working over another clean bowl in which to catch the white, carefully stick your thumbs in the crack you've made and gently open the eggshell into 2 halves. Immediately transfer the entire contents of the egg into one half. Then transfer it back into the second half.

As you go back and forth, allow some of the white to slide out into the catch bowl. Do that a few times until mainly the yolk is left. If you keep doing this, the yolk will eventually break, and this game will cease being fun. So stop when it looks like you've separated most of the white out and the yolk is still intact.

Omelets

Omelets are just scrambled eggs with style, turned out all fluffy and elegant and often filled with good stuff. They're also easy. In truth, the only thing you need to know how to do is how to buy a nonstick pan.

The recipe below will feed two people; 2 eggs cooked in an 8- or 9-inch pan will produce a perfect meal for one.

SERVES 2 / WINE PAIRING: Champagne or other Sparkling Wine

4 large eggs
$1/4$ teaspoon kosher salt
$1/4$ teaspoon freshly ground black pepper
1 tablespoon unsalted butter

> Beat the eggs with the salt and pepper in a bowl with a fork until blended.

> Heat the butter in a 10-inch nonstick frying pan over a medium-high flame. When the butter begins to turn a golden brown color, pour in the eggs. Let them sit there for about 5 seconds until you see the edges start to set. Then, using a wooden spoon, stir the eggs for 5 to 10 seconds, until they start to thicken and scramble.

> To finish cooking, pull the egg from one side of the pan in toward the center. Then tilt the pan toward that side to let the uncooked egg run along the edges into the pan. Do the same thing on another side and keep doing this until no more uncooked egg runs to the edges. By this time the omelet should be completely set and moist but not runny on top.

> Use the spoon or a spatula to peek at the bottom of the omelet. Although French tradition has it that an omelet should be uncolored, I disagree: The omelet tastes better if it is a little browned. So let it cook until it has developed a bit of color.

> Use the spoon or a spatula to fold the back third of the omelet over the center. Fold the front third over and slide the omelet out onto a plate. Cut it in half and serve hot.

+ *VARIATION:* Omelet with Dill, Scallion, and Fontina
Beat the eggs with the salt and pepper, and add 1 tablespoon coarsely chopped fresh dill and 1 chopped scallion. When the eggs are just set, sprinkle with a scant $1/4$ cup grated Fontina cheese. Fold the omelet as in the recipe above.

+ *VARIATION:* Omelet with Tomato, Oregano, and Feta Cheese
Quarter a plum tomato and cut out the pulp, leaving 4 strips of tomato meat; slice crosswise. Beat the eggs with the salt and pepper, and add $1/4$ teaspoon dried oregano. Toss the tomato in 1 teaspoon olive oil and a pinch of salt over medium heat for 30 seconds, just to warm. Transfer to a plate and make the omelet as in the recipe above. When the eggs are just set, sprinkle with the tomato and a scant $1/4$ cup crumbled feta cheese. Fold as in the recipe above.

+ *VARIATION:* **Omelet with Asparagus and Parmigiano**
Steam 2 trimmed asparagus stalks over boiling water until tender, about 2 minutes. Cut into 2-inch pieces. Toss the asparagus over medium heat in 2 teaspoons olive oil and a pinch of salt for 30 seconds. Transfer to a plate. Beat the eggs with the salt and pepper, and add 2 tablespoons grated Parmigiano-Reggiano. Cook the omelet as in the recipe above, adding the asparagus when the eggs are set.

+ *VARIATION:* **Omelet with Fresh Herbs and Prosciutto**
Beat the eggs with the salt and pepper, and add 2 tablespoons chopped mixed soft herbs such as parsley, tarragon, and chives. When the eggs are set, scatter over 2 thin slices prosciutto, torn into pieces. Fold the omelet as in the recipe above.

French toast

The idea behind French toast is that it's made with stale bread. The French name is *pain perdu,* or "lost bread," meaning bread that would otherwise have been thrown out if not eaten as French toast. The bread is soaked in egg and milk to bring it back to life. In my experience most people don't have stale bread hanging around; I buy fresh challah (a rich, eggy bread that's usually sold in a braided loaf) especially to make French toast. So I've dispensed with the milk. You've got to eat it right out of the pan or it will get dry. Figure on getting 1½ to 2 slices of toast per egg.

SERVES 2

3 large eggs
Pinch of fine salt
¼ teaspoon pure vanilla extract
3 tablespoons unsalted butter
5 to 6 slices fresh challah
Confectioners' sugar, maple syrup, or jam, for serving

> In a large bowl, whisk together the eggs, salt, and vanilla.

> Heat 1 tablespoon butter in a 9-inch frying pan over a medium flame until melted. Working with 1 piece at a time, turn 2 challah slices in the egg so that it soaks the bread. Put both slices in the pan. Cook until lightly browned on one side, 2 to 3 minutes. Turn with a spatula and cook for another 2 minutes, or until browned on the second side. Serve up those 2 slices immediately and continue cooking, using 1 tablespoon butter for each batch, until you've used all the bread and egg. Serve sprinkled with confectioners' sugar or with maple syrup or jam.

Sweet oven-baked pancake with lemon

This pancake is really impressive; it bakes up tall and beautiful, like a crown, and falls in the center. The batter can also be made in a blender: Just combine all of the ingredients and buzz until smooth. The buttermilk adds a nice tang—brings out the lemon—but milk will substitute nicely.

SERVES 3 TO 4

3 large eggs
3/4 cup buttermilk or whole milk
3/4 cup all-purpose flour
3 tablespoons granulated sugar
Pinch of salt
Grated zest of 1 lemon
3 tablespoons unsalted butter
2 tablespoons confectioners' sugar
Lemon wedges, for serving

> Preheat the oven to 425°F.

> Beat the eggs in a medium bowl with a fork or whisk. Beat in the buttermilk or milk. Sprinkle the flour over the top and beat that in, too. Beat in the granulated sugar, salt, and lemon zest.

> Heat the butter over a medium flame in a 9-inch ovenproof pan (cast-iron is good) until melted. Then continue cooking until the butter turns light golden brown (don't cook it further—it burns quickly). Pour in the batter, put the pan in the oven, and bake until the pancake is puffed and brown, 18 to 20 minutes. Remove from the oven and sprinkle with the confectioners' sugar. Cut into wedges and serve immediately, with squeezes of lemon juice.

Acknowledgments

My thanks to my co-conspirator Stephanie Lyness, for her taste, skill, and boundless enthusiasm for collaboration; to my brilliant and exceptionally well-dressed editor, Chris Pavone; to Jane Treuhaft, Marysarah Quinn, Mark McCauslin, Felix Gregorio, Tammy Blake, and the whole Clarkson Potter team; to Helene Silverman for the crisp and beautiful design; to Bill Bettencourt and his incomparable chefs and stylists Megan Schlow, Ronnie Freedman, and Dawn Sinkowski; to Julio Santiago and Oleg Rabinovich of ArtSee Eyewear New York; to Paul Rousseas of Paul Smith New York; and to the makeup genius Rachel Pagani, without whom America would be sad.

To my literary guru at the William Morris Agency, Jay Mandel, and everybody there who has worked so hard and so smart for me: Betsy Berg, Brian Dubin, Jeff Googel, Andy McNichol, and Adam Sher.

To Bob Myman, the lifesaver; to Frank Selvaggi and Lea DiPerna; to my whip-smartest friend Elizabeth Holland for her business acumen; to Nancy Maniscalco, owner and missionary of the brilliant Nancy's Wines for Food in New York City; to the abusive older brothers I never thought I'd have— Jai Rodriguez, Thom Filicia, Kyan Douglas, and Carson Kressley; to the bums and gypsies on the *Queer Eye* crew who always knew where to find that little something, that inky-dink, at the nineteenth hour; to Richard Babcock for giving me my first great job at *Chicago* magazine, and to Penny Pollack for teaching me how to review restaurants; to Scott Omelianuk for bringing me to *Esquire,* and to David Granger for so many sensitive edits there; to Terry Sullivan and the Steadfast Monica; to visionaries David Collins, Michael Williams, and Dave Metzler, who nurtured an improbable dream from the South End to the Emmy Awards, and to everybody at Scout Productions; to the chefs who have been so kind and helpful to me over the past three years—in ways both small and large—among them Bobby Flay, Mario Batali, Eric Ripert, Sara Moulton, Ming Tsai, Tyler Florence, Suvir Saran, Jacques Pépin, Todd English, Scott Campbell, and Scotty Conant; to Jason and Rachel Perlow, Dana Cowin, Barbara Fairchild, Alton Brown, Max McCalman, Jeffrey Steingarten, and everybody at *Iron Chef America,* especially Bruce Seidel; to all the people who have watched *QE* and who have written us with their inspiring stories; to Ted and Nancy for that long-ago Beef Wellington in Broad Ripple; to Mom, Dad, Lisa, and Mike, who taught me about words, integrity, and the ever-expanding beauty of family, and to the always-magical Megan, Cole, and Tate.

Index